From an
Outhouse
to the
White House
and Tennessee
A Primer on Arkansas Words and Ways

Wallace O. Chariton
caricatures by Bo McCord

Wordware Publishing, Inc.

All inquiries for volume purchases of this book should be addressed to
Wordware Publishing, Inc., at the above address. Telephone inquiries may
be made by calling:
(214) 423-0090

Table of Contents

Dedication

This one is dedicated to Glen P. Owen who, many years ago, introduced me to the wonderful simplicity of country language when he said I was like a catfish, all mouth and no brains.

A special thanks . . .

to the listeners of Kevin McCarthy's show on KLIF, 570 AM, Dallas, Texas.

A Brief Introduction

There's an old saying that goes, "He went from the outhouse to the penthouse." Basically, that means someone who started from humble beginnings made it all the way to the big time. Well, Bill Clinton has now gone one step further; he's made it from his "outhouse" beginning in Hope, Arkansas, all the way to the nation's penthouse.

With the new administration will come change, that's inevitable. Quicker than a minnow can swim a dipper there's going to be more Southern folks dippin' their snout in the government trough than there has been in a long time. And that can spell trouble for anyone not tuned into the words and ways of the South, particularly those of Arkansas and Tennessee. The American people are going to be introduced to Southern ways that will be new and certainly different because one of the popular philosophies of the South is simply, "We don't give a damn how you do it up North."

One area of change will be in language usage. In their November 30, 1992 issue, the editors of *Newsweek* magazine proclaimed that "preppyisms" are dead and that, ". . . America should brace for some of his [Clinton's] singularly Arkansan expressions." While the editors of *Newsweek* are certainly correct about a language shift, I would argue that Clinton will not use "singularly Arkansan" expressions. The truth is, after years of study and research, I've found very few sayings and expressions that are unique to Arkansas. For example, *Newsweek* sighted five different expressions, and while they are all Southern sayings, not one of them is unique to Arkansas. Not by a long shot.

One part of the *Newsweek* article partially inspired this book. The editors quoted Clinton as saying, "down to the lick log" but reported that the derivation was unclear, *even to Clinton staffers.* The problem thus presented is that if Clinton's own people don't know what he's saying, the rest of the nation (and the world, for that matter) may be in for a long four years of confusion. The most popular phrase in Washington may become either "What'd he say?" or "What in the hell does that mean?"

As a public service to help non-Southerners through the verbal fog, I decided to put together this little primer of Southern words and ways with an emphasis on Arkansas and Tennessee. This, of course, is not the definitive Southern lexicon because that would take more than four years to compile. I'll start working on the definitive version, however, and if it looks like Clinton has a chance at reelection, I'll try to get it published.

In the meantime, this primer should help, and hopefully entertain, anyone wanting to know about "talkin' Southern." You'll notice that the book is in three sections. Section One is a sort of dictionary full of popular Southern sayings, words that are unique to or heavily used in the South, plus an occasional explanation where necessary, such as for "lick log." Section Two is more of a pronunciation dictionary that can prove invaluable for the endless number of coat-tail riders who all of a sudden will want to sound like they were raised on grits and gravy. Also included are the general rules for talking Southern. Section Three contains such valuable information as the words to *Dixie*, a list of acceptable Southern manners, Southern bumper stickers, and Southern proverbs.

If you have a favorite Southern saying that isn't included in this collection, you're welcome to send it to me care of: Wordware Publishing, Inc., 1506 Capital Ave., Plano, Texas 75074. If the Clinton reign lasts more than four years, your contribution will be included in the ultimate Southern Dictionary, due out as quickly as possible after the December 1996 election.

Till we meet again, keep your wagon between the ditches and stay away from my lick log.

Wallace O. Chariton

P.S.: To the good people of Arkansas and Tennessee, remember I didn't invent this stuff, I just reported it.

SECTION ONE

A Primer on Arkansas and Tennessee Words and Ways

CORNBREAD: Arkansas wedding cake

A: In the South, "A" is frequently used to add emphasis. "It was a-hailin' and a-rainin' and a-lightnin', but I still went fishin'. • A also means "of" in the South. "What kind a pickup is that?"

A.B.C.: Alcoholic Beverage Commission, which controls what you drink, sort of, in Arkansas. In some parts of the South, the A.B.C. actually operates stores where whiskey can be purchased.

A LOT: Forty-leven dozen. "Bubba has tried to get Betty Lou to go out with him forty-leven dozen times but she's stood her ground so far." In practice, forty-leven dozen is used to mean any large amount. In fact, forty-leven dozen is 4,011 dozen, or 48,132.

A LOT OF FISH: A mess of, which is an undetermined amount that usually means a stringer full, a Styrofoam ice chest full, or enough to feed all the kinfolk who are comin' to supper.

A LOT OF TIME HAS ELAPSED: A lot of scum has been scraped off the pond since then.

ABILITY, NATURAL: He learned how to do that while he was still in the oven. Oven, in this case, means womb, so the saying translates into, "He was born with the ability."

ABOUT TO: Fixin' to in the South. "I'm fixin' to cut the grass."

ABOUT TO LEAVE: He's gettin ready to git.

ABOUT TO LOSE: You're circling the drain, implying that you are about to go down it.

ABSOLUTELY: Would a ten-foot chicken lay a big egg? • Is a pig's butt pork? *See also Yes*

ACCEPT YOUR FATE: Bloom where you're planted.

ACCOMPANY: Come go with me.

ACCURATE AS: A weather vane. No matter which way the wind blows, the weather vane will always be right.

ACCUSATION: That's a skunk tellin' a possum his breath stinks.

ACTING FOOLISH: You're askin' a blind man to tell you which horse to buy.

ACTING STRANGE: He's acting like he's got too many rats in his outhouse.

ACTION, WITHOUT RESULTS: She did a heap a stirring but she didn't get many biscuits.

ADROIT: She's got more moves than a possum on roller skates.

ADVICE: When you're up to your neck in manure, don't open your mouth. • Never put all your eggs in one basket or all your whiskey in one woman. • Don't change horses (or diapers) in mid-stream.

AGITATED: He gave my crank a good pull.

AGREEABLE: I can dance to that tune.

ALIMONY: Is like buying oats for somebody else's mule.

ALL OR NOTHING: It's the whole hog or no hog.

ALL THE WAY: Clear to. "He went clear to the county line tryin' to outrun the sheriff."

ALL WORK, NO PLAY: All hominy and no ham.

ALMOST: Like to. "I like to forgot my anniversary." • Pert near. "I pert near forgot to buy some beer." • Nearly bout. "I nearly bout got slapped when I tried to kiss that girl."

ALMOST FINISHED: We're hoein' in the short rows.

ALTERNATIVE: There are more ways to kill a cat than choking him on warm butter.

ALWAYS TALKING: He don't ever fall on his mouth.

AMAZING: That'll blow your gown up over your head.

AMBITIOUS: He's whittlin' on a big limb.

AMBITIOUS, OVERLY: He keeps his wick turned up high, which basically means he's trying to be a shining light.

AMEN CORNER: A pew near the pulpit, usually reserved for the most devout (and vocal) members of the congregation.

ANCESTRY: Bark of the family tree.

ANEMIC: Tick proof, which means he's so anemic, if he cut off a toe he'd have to get a transfusion before he could bleed.

ANGERS: That tweaks my beak.

ANGRY: Foamin' at the mouth mad. • He's so mad he can't spit straight.

ANIMAL TRAINER, EXPERT: He could train a cow to hook herself up to an automatic milking machine.

ANIMALS: Critters, if they are friendly, varmints if they ain't.

ANXIOUS: As a Tennessee country preacher after a fat fryer.

ANXIOUS BENCH: A special bench in the front of a church reserved for those who are real "anxious" about something.

ANXIETY, HIGH: He's wound up tighter'n a two-dollar watch.

ANYONE CAN DO IT: In describing something that anyone, even an idiot, ought to be able to do he said, "Even a blind hog can find an acorn."

APOLOGY, LARGE: He ate crow, feathers, beak and all.

APPEARANCE, BAD: He looks like he was pulled through a knothole backwards. • She looks like some corn field is missing a scarecrow.

APPEARANCE, DECEIVING: Just because a chicken has wings don't mean she can fly.

APPREHENSIVE: As a cow waitin' to be milked on a cold morning ('cause she knows his hands ain't gonna be warm).

ARGUMENT, STUPID: That's about as dumb as two bald-headed men fighting over a fine-tooth comb.

ARGUMENTATIVE: He'd argue with a wooden Indian.

ARID LAND: That land has about as much water as a secretarial pool.

ARKANSAS: The Natural State; chicken capital of the world; land of tall girls and virgin pines, where there's plenty of hills, thrills, and stills. The only state mentioned in the Bible. "Noah looked out the Ark an' saw . . . " The proper pronunciation is Arkan-SAW although Ar-KAN-zus was once considered acceptable. The pronunciation issue was settled in 1881 by a special committee appointed by the state legislature.

ARKANSAS PERSON: There is some controversy over exactly what to call a person in Arkansas. Arkies was once used but it is not common today. Some people say Ar-KAN-san and others use Arkansasan, but a lot of the natives refer to themselves as Arkansawers.

ARMADILLO: Possum on the half shell. During Mr. Hoover's great depression, armadillos were known as "Hoover Hogs" because they were about as close as poor folks got to real pork.

AROUND THE HOUSE: Around the place.

ARRANGE: Fix. "Would you fix the dinner table."

ARROGANT: He can strut sitting down.

ARTIST, POOR: He couldn't draw a conclusion.

ASHTRAY: Arkansas fingernail clipping holder.

ASKING FOR TROUBLE: You're imitating a lightning rod.

ASSEMBLED, POORLY: Jerry rigged or Southern engineered.

ASSIGNMENT, DIFFICULT: You might as well ask me to change bulbs in a lightnin' bug.

ASSOCIATED: In cahoots with or hunkered down with.

AT HIS MERCY: He's got me by the short hairs.

AT MOST: At farthest. "Bubba, that mule ought'n to cost more than $30 or $40 at farthest.

ATHLETE, INEPT: He plays like he ought to be in a game where the mothers make the uniforms.

ATHLETE, STUPID: He can do anything with a football except autograph it.

ATTACKED: Like grandma after a chicken snake with a chunk of firewood.

ATTEMPT: Try your hand at. "I'm gonna try my hand at weldin' one of these days."

ATTENTION GETTER: That'll get your attention faster than a cross-eyed man at a turkey shoot.

ATTRACTED TO: He took to that like a chicken to a new pie pan. Because a new pie pan is shiny, a chicken likes to peck out of one so she can see her reflection, or so they say.

ATTRACTIVE, SOMEWHAT: Leans toward. "Bubba leans toward handsome."

AUTOMATIC: Oughta-matic. A type of transmission for your pickup or a rifle that makes huntin' easy.

AUTOMOBILE DEALERSHIP: House (Ford house) or place (Chevrolet place).

AVERAGE QUALITY: It's just fair to middlin.

AVOID: You better plow around that stump.

AWHILE: A spell. "It's been quite a spell since anyone in Arkansas got arrested for operating an illegal still."

AWKWARD: As a cow gigging fish.

B **BABY:** A sucker that ought to get an even break. In the South, babies are frequently referred to as "it" even if you know the gender. "It looks just like its daddy."

BABY COWS: Only the greenest of greenhorns (or the silliest of Yankees) would say "baby cows." They are calves.

BACK PAIN: Down in the back. "Billy Fred is shore down in the back after liftin' that engine out of his pickup."

BACK LOG: The large log placed at the back of the stove to provide flames for cooking and heat for sleeping. The back log smolders all night and even if it burns up completely, there are usually enough hot embers to start a fire the next morning.

BACKWARDS: Southerners rarely use the word backwards. They prefer "bassackwards" or "you got the hind part before."

BAD DAY: If today was a fish, I'd throw it back.

BALD: I've seen more hair on a crystal ball. • He looks like his hair was parted by lightning.

BALING WIRE: Wire designed for baling hay which is used to repair everything from false teeth to windmills.

BANGING: Like a screen door during a picnic at an orphanage.

BANK ROLL, ARKANSAS STYLE: A roll of money where the top and bottom bills are real and the rest are newspaper.

BANKER, TIGHT: He gives you the same amount of credit as an Arkansas sharecropper gets in a New Orleans whorehouse.

BARBECUE: Most Southerners believe that if they don't get a barbecue fix at least once a week they might go into a barbecue coma. In Arkansas and Tennessee, pork is the favored meat, but beef, chicken, and possum aren't far behind.

BARBECUE SAUCE: Correction fluid, 'cause it has covered up more mistakes than all the maternity dresses ever made.

BASEBALL-TYPE CAP: Gimmie cap in the South. The baseball type cap got its name "gimmie" from the fact that feed stores, implement dealers, and other merchants once gave them away for advertising purposes. Although most people now sell "gimmie" hats, a real Southerner wouldn't think of buying one.

BASHFUL: It makes him blush every time he remembers he was in bed naked with a woman the day he was born.

BASS, LARGE: Any bass over ten pounds (that has not been filled with two or three pounds of lead sinkers) is a "hawg."

BATHROOM LIMB: A tree limb low enough that you can sit down on it and do your business.

BATTERY, POWERFUL: It'd jump start a nuclear submarine.

BE CAREFUL: Don't plow too close to the cotton.

BE HAPPY WITH WHAT YOU GOT: Count your blessings.

BE HOME EARLY: Don't let sundown catch you not home.

BE PATIENT: Don't count the crop till it's in the barn.

BE PREPARED: If you're gonna run with the big dogs, be ready to hike your leg in tall grass.

BE QUIET: Hush your mouth, a favorite saying of Southern mothers.

BE SATISFIED: If you get an egg, don't worry about whether or not the chicken likes you.

BE SPECIFIC: Don't tell me how the still works, give me a drink.

BE STILL: Get your nest built.

BE SURE YOU'RE RIGHT: Davy Crockett said, "Be sure you're right, then go ahead."

BEANS: Arkansas strawberries.

BEAT: Give him a what-for lesson.

BEATEN, GOOD: He pounded my head so far down I had to unzip my pants to blow my nose. • He whipped the living daylights out of me.

BECOME: Make. "I believe Betty is gonna make a hair dresser."

BED SPRINGS, USED: Arkansas television antenna, when nailed to the roof of a cabin.

BELIEVE ME: If I say a razorback sow can play a fiddle, you can rosin up the bow and clear the floor for dancing.

BET: Risk. "I'd risk all my egg money on you not being able to eat six soda crackers in less than a minute."

BIBLE CAKE: A cake made from a recipe written in scriptures. For instance, for eggs it would be Jeremiah 17:11, "As the partridge sitteth on eggs, and hatcheth them not." Any ingredient needed for a Bible cake, a favorite at church socials, can be specified by a different scripture.

BIG BUILDING: It's big enough to hold an indoor deer hunt.

BIG PERSON: It'd take a committee of three men and two dogs just to look him over. • He could go bear hunting with a switch and give the switch to the bear.

BILL OF FARE, ARKANSAS STYLE: Coon 'n collards • owl 'n okra • chitlins 'n turnip greens • goobers 'n sweet 'taters • baked possum and poke salit • squirrel and dumplings • fried coon and blackeye gravy • 'taters and chitlins

BISCUITS, LARGE: Cathead biscuits, which means they're as big as the head of a cat and perfect for sopping syrup.

BLACK TAPE: Tape used to fix anything from hemlines to electric lines.

BLACKBERRY WINTER: A cold snap that comes after the blackberries have bloomed in the spring. Also called dogwood winter.

BLACKSTRAP MOLASSES: *See Sorghum*

BLEEDING: Like a stuck pig • Like a castrated elephant.

BLESS HIS HEART: This is a magical Southern phrase that allows you to say something really tacky about someone without seeming to be tacky. "That ol' Bubba, he ain't got the sense God gave a screwdriver, bless his heart."

BLINKING EYES, QUICKLY: He's eyelids were batting like they were on a Baptist preacher in the front row at a striptease.

BLIVIT: The sound made when you put ten pounds of manure in a five-pound sack and hit someone with it.

BLOW, MISDIRECTED: A mislick. " Jim Bob swung a hoe handle at the jukebox, but thank goodness it was a mislick."

BOILED PEANUTS: In some places in the South, especially Georgia, boiled (pronounced bowled) peanuts are considered a delicacy. To boil your own, use fresh, uncooked (green) peanuts and leave 'em in the shell. Boil slowly in salted water in a heavy pot for about four hours, drain, and serve. Use caution when opening the shells of boiled peanuts because all the water may not have drained out.

BOIS D' ARC: Bow-dark or Osage orange, an extremely hard wood that is perfect for fence posts.

BOLD AS: A 300-pound cat burglar.

BORED: A wooden Indian in a forest fire would have more fun than I'm having.

BORING: As a fishing trip with a game warden.

BORN LOSER: If he'd a been a dog on Noah's ark, he would a gotten both fleas.

BOSS: Big hog at the trough • The tail twister.

BOWLEGGED: He couldn't catch a pig in a ditch.

BRAGGING: He's struttin' his okra, which means you could fertilize 100 acres of bottom land with what he's spreadin' around.

BRAVE: He's got more guts than a fiddle factory. • He's got more nerve than a broken tooth.

BREAKFAST: The most important meal of the day 'cause if you ain't home by then, you're in big trouble.

BREATH, STRONG: His breath is strong enough he can't wear his false teeth 'cause they might dissolve.

BRIGHT PERSON: He's so bright we have to put him in the closet to get the sun to come up.

BROKE: I was so broke, I could only buy one slice of bacon. I'd hang it up by a string and the younguns would jump up and grab it in their mouth to slide down slow and easy to grease their gums enough to fool their stomach. • I'm so broke if a fat goose cost a dollar I couldn't afford to kiss a hummingbird.

BROWN BAG IT: When a Northerner "brown bags it" he takes his lunch to work in a brown paper sack. When a Southerner "brown bags it" he takes his sippin' whiskey to a juke joint in a brown paper sack.

BRUSH ARBOR: A temporary shelter used for revivals.

BRUSH, THICK: The snakes had to climb trees to look out. In the South, a laurel or rhododendron thicket is a "woolly-head."

BUCK-TOOTHED: He could eat a watermelon through a picket fence and not get a gum wet.

BUMPKIN: He just arrived on a load of cordwood.

BUNCHED UP: Like wild turkeys in a hailstorm.

BUSINESS: Bidness. "Bubba has gone into the weldin' bidness."

BUSINESS ADVICE: Don't sign nuthin' in a neon light's glow.

BUST, LARGE: The 8th and 9th wonders of the world.

BUST, SMALL: She could put her bra on backwards and not notice the difference.

BUSY: I'm catching 'em faster than I can string 'em.

BUSY AS: Grandma with one hoe and two snakes • As a pair of jumper cables at an Arkansas funeral.

BUY A NEW VEHICLE: Trade cars (or pickups). "I think I'm gonna go down to the Ford place and see if I can trade cars."

 CALL ME: Give me a holler • Call the house.

CALM THEM DOWN: Gentle the hogs.

CALM TOWN: "It's a hotbed of tranquility," as Edward D. Stone said of his hometown, Fayetteville, Arkansas.

CALM: As the bottom of an empty post hole.

CANE STALKS: Arkansas firecrackers. When green cane stalks are pitched into a fire, they will "pop" loudly at each joint.

CARE TO: See fit. "If you see fit, we'll go hunting."

CAREFUL AS: A nudist crawling through a barbed wire fence.

CARP: A Southern game fish that is fun to catch but which is not considered good to eat. However, if you must try here's a good recipe. Clean the carp thoroughly and cut off the head. Baste liberally with a lemon-butter sauce, place on a cedar shingle about fourteen inches long, and put into an oven. Bake for thirty minutes, remove from oven, throw away the carp, eat the shingle.

CARPENTER, POOR: The only way he can keep from hitting his thumb is if his wife holds the nail.

CARRY: Tote, lug, heft, or bring it in the South.

CARRY THROUGH: You don't get lard unless you boil the hog.

CATFISH: A bottom-dwelling, scavenging Southern game fish that's said to be all mouth and no brains, which is why folks in the South often compare politicians to catfish.

CATTLE, THIN: Those cows are so thin we had to tie 'em together with rawhide to keep 'em from fallin' apart.

CAUGHT: Like a chicken snake in a picket fence, which refers to a chicken snake slithering through a fence to eat an egg, then discovering he can't crawl back through until the egg is digested.

CAUGHT IN THE MIDDLE: Like a redneck between two city lawyers.

CAUTIOUS: As a young rooster in an old rooster's pen. Old roosters tend to be real protective of their territory.

CELEBRATE: We're gonna shoot an anvil, which is an ol' country practice of loading an anvil with powder and setting it off to celebrate an event such as New Year's Eve.

CELEBRATING EARLY: You're cackling before the egg is laid.

CHALLENGE: Tryin' to turn a pair of boots back into a cow.

CHANCES, POOR: You got two chances, slim and fat. • You ain't got an ice cube's chance in an oven. • You ain't got any more chance than a kerosene cat in hell with gasoline drawers on.

CHANGED HUSBANDS: She found a new dasher for the churn.

CHANGES HIS MIND FREQUENTLY: Got the mind of a dung heap beetle.

CHARACTER: If you don't stand for something, you'll fall for anything.

CHARMING: He could charm the chrome off a bumper hitch.

CHEAP: As an umbrella in a drought.

CHEAP ISN'T ALWAYS BEST: The cheapest oats are ones that have already been through the horse.

CHEAPSKATE: His idea of charity is offering $500 to the family of the Unknown Soldier.

CHEWING TOBACCO: Chew backey. Chewing tobacco is an art. When you start you'll notice a collection of tobacco juice in your mouth that you have to do something with, and spitting it out is much preferred to swallowing it. With practice you'll be spitting well enough to drown house flies on the wing. However, always remember the three rules of chewing: 1. Practice a lot before trying to drink a beer while chewing. 2. Always spit downwind. 3. Around other chewers, never drink from any can you didn't personally open. *See also Pickup Aerodynamics*

CHEWING TOBACCO UNIT OF MEASURE: Plug or chaw.

CHICKEN: Yard bird • Arkansas pheasant.

CHICKEN, GOOD: She could hatch a petrified dinosaur egg. One Arkansas chicken was so good she starved to death trying to hatch a lost golf ball.

CHICKEN, POOR: She couldn't lay an egg if she was sittin' on a vacuum cleaner and it was running.

CHICKEN, SOUTHERN FRIED: What God would eat if they had chickens in heaven. To prepare properly, start with a Southern chicken (they're the most tender) and cut into manageable pieces. Remove the wing from the breast, cut the breast into two pieces, and separate the drumstick from the thigh. Dip in your own special batter and deep fry until golden brown and every single drop of blood is gone. When prepared properly, by a Southerner, fried chicken will "straighten your teeth, smooth your skin, and make childbirth a pleasure." Because Southerners know that fingers were invented before forks, fried chicken is definitely a finger food.

CHIGGERS: Red bugs. Pound for pound, the chigger is the meanest critter on the face of the earth. They love to bite in places that you can't scratch in public.

CHILD, ARKANSAS STYLE: A handle jiggler. Whenever an indoor toilet doesn't shut off properly, an Arkansas mother will look straight at one of the kids and say, "Somebody go jiggle that handle."

CHILD, GROWN 'N GONE: The chick has flown the coup.

CHILD, WORTHLESS: His mother should have stayed a virgin, which is how Lillian Carter, mother of Jimmy and Billy, once described herself.

CHINKING: Mud or clay, mixed with straw, that was used to fill the cracks between logs in cabins. Chinking works very well until it becomes extremely dry and starts to drop out in chunks. When enough of the chinking falls out, the cabin is naturally air-conditioned, both in summer and winter.

CHITLINS: Also called chitterlings. These are small squares of hog intestines that are deep fried until crisp. A favorite Southern dish, although some folks who cook 'em don't actually eat them. According to a Southern legend, when cooking chitlins the smell is so bad it drives all the flies out of the house and keeps 'em out for up to two weeks, which may explain why you rarely see flies around mountain cabins.

CIDER, FERMENTED: Arkansas or Tennessee champagne.

CIVIL WAR: Never say "Civil War" in the South. It's either The War Between the States, The War of Northern Aggression, or The War for Southern Independence.

CLARIFY: Crack that nut a little closer to the meat. • Slice a little more fat off the hog.

CLEAN LIVING: In the South, clean livin' means live your life so the Secret Service could tap your phone and then play the tapes in church and you wouldn't be the least bit embarrassed.

CLEAN UP: Sweep the yard. Mountain folks don't have much grass in their front yard so to clean up around the place, they just sweep up everything, dirt, leaves, trash, twigs, bones, and all.

CLIMB A TREE: Shinny up it or skin it. "Bubba, shinny up that tree and get the cat down 'fore he falls and hurts hisself."

CLINGS: Like a tick to a runnin' dog's ear. • Like a cocklebur to a mule's tail.

The Clintons, first family of Arkansas

CLINTON, WILLIAM JEFFERSON: Beal CLINT-un, Prez-a-dent. Any self-respecting Southern boy named William Jefferson ought to be called Billy Jeff, B.J., Willie, or Bubba. Hillary (Hill'ry) Clinton, Bill's wife, is now First Woman.

CLOROX BOTTLE, EMPTY: An empty Clorox bottle is one of the most versatile tools in Arkansas. It can be used as is for a flower vase or an emergency gas can; it can be sealed and used for a trot line float; you can cut the bottom straight off and use it for a funnel or seedling cover; you can cut the bottom off at an angle and use it for a water bailer or grain scoop.

CLOSE: *See Distance*

CLOSE CALL: I didn't lose nuthin' but a little hide and a lot of confidence.

CLOSE TOGETHER: As two fleas on a frozen dog.

CLOTHES, DIRTY: He don't believe in wearing 'em out by washing 'em.

CLOTHES, INSIDE OUT: Wrong sideouten. "Bubba likes to wear T-shirts wrong sideouten to keep the outside clean."

CLOTHES, TIGHT: She fills up them clothes like hot wax fills up a candle mold. Her clothes were tight as a first-day bride's. *See also Jeans, Tight*

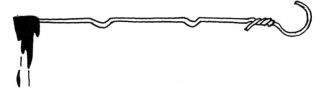

COAT HANGER: Arkansas dipstick.

COFFEE, BAD: Tastes like coal squeezin's or stump water.

COFFEE, STRONG: You could drive a nail with it.

COFFEE, WEAK: It's weaker than well water.

COLD: It was so cold my teeth chattered and they were in a jar on the dresser. • It was cold as a knothole on the North Pole.

COLD ENOUGH: To freeze the balls off a pool table.

COMMITTED: The different between being committed and just involved is the difference between having bacon and eggs. The chicken is involved; the pig is totally committed.

COMMITTED, SOMEWHAT: He ain't on the bandwagon but he's running beside it.

COMMITTED, TOTALLY: Bound and determined. "That Bubba is bound and determined to open a septic tank business."

COMMON: As pigs in Arkansas • As guitar pickers in Tennessee • As cows in Texas

COMMOTION: Ruckus. "They raised a bigger ruckus than a lizard in a pile of dry leaves."

COMPANY, FAILING: On its last legs and they're wobbling.

COMPATIBLE: They go together like ugly and possum.

COMPETITION: Minnie Pearl's motto is: "If you can't beat 'em, confuse 'em."

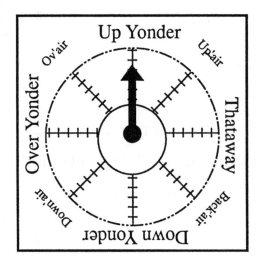

COMPASS, ARKANSAS STYLE

COMPLAINED BITTERLY: They squealed like a pig caught under a gate, as Bill Clinton said.

COMPLICATION: We got a fly in the ointment.

COMPLIMENT, SORT OF: She's a lot nicer than she is ugly.

CONCEITED: He thinks the sun comes up just to hear him crow.

CONFUSED: He's as confused as a woodpecker in a petrified forest. • She don't know if she's washin' or hangin' out. • He was so confused he was winding his butt and scratching his watch. • For confused, Bill Clinton used, "He don't know come here from sic 'em." See also One-Holer for how to confuse an Arkansas redneck.

CONFUSED AS: A termite in a yo-yo.

CONNIPTION FIT: It's important to know the difference between a conniption fit and a hissey fit. A conniption fit is a sort of tantrum that you throw whenever someone does something to you. "Bubba had a conniption fit when I dropped the Evinrude on his ingrown toenail." A snot-slingin' conniption fit is twice as bad as a plain one, and a foamin' at the mouth conniption fit is the worst of all and usually indicates blood is about to be spilled. A hissey fit is a tantrum you throw when you don't get your way. "Lizza Lou threw a hissey fit when her daddy wouldn't buy her a new car." A wall-eyed hissey fit would be a lot worse and a snot-slinging, foot stomping hissey fit is the worst of all.

CONSERVATIVE: He never plants more garden than his wife can hoe.

CONSIDERATE: He holds the door open when his wife carries in the groceries.

CONSTIPATED: I feel like I swallowed a stopper.

CONTRARY: She's so full of contrariness, if she fell in the creek and drowned she'd float upstream.

COOK, GOOD: She could make a meal out of a bone's smell.

COOK, INEPT: She'd put dark meat in her chicken salad, which is something you just don't do in the South. Ever.

COOK, POOR: She can scorch water tryin' to boil it.

COONIN' A LOG: When the water is so high you have to sit down and sort of frog hop across a stream on a footlog.

COOPERATION: We all can't play the same saxophone but we can all play the same song.

COORDINATION: He could bait a hook while standing up in a boat during a storm and never spill a drop of beer. • He can roll a cigarette while standing up in the back of a pickup goin' ninety miles an hour. • She could hold twins while ironing in high heels and never miss the spit can on the ironing board.

COORDINATION, POOR: He has to pull over to the side of the road and come to a dead stop before he can pick his nose.

CORDWOOD: Cordwood is a piece of firewood about 24 inches long, which fits nicely in most fireplaces. If you have a stack of wood four feet high, four feet wide, and eight feet long, you have a cord of wood.

CORNBREAD: Arkansas wedding cake.

CORNBREAD AND CLABBER: Arkansas malt, made by crumbling cornbread into a glass of buttermilk.

COTTON GRADES: *See Quality, Fair*

COUNTRY BOY, SMART: He may not eat possum, coon, armadillo, or jackrabbit but he knows where to find 'em if another depression breaks out.

COURTHOUSE BENCH: Liar's bench. Old-timers sit on a courthouse bench to spit and whittle while they tell lies all day.

COURTING: Sparkin'. In the South when two youngsters are sweet on each other, a smart mother will have 'em shell beans so they can get some work done while sparkin'. That same mother wouldn't want 'em huskin' corn 'cause that's done in the barn.

COW BIRD: A small white bird that spends all its time pickin' ticks off cows or peckin' through manure, which is why they are frequently compared to politicians.

COW, WILD: She could go through a barbed wire fence like a fallin' tree through a cobweb.

COWARD: You couldn't melt him down and pour him into a fight.

CRACKED OPEN: Like an egg laid by a tall chicken.

CRAFTY: She could spit through a broom and not get a straw wet.

CRAVE: Got a hankerin' or a hurtin' for it.

CRAYFISH: Crawdads or Arkansas lobsters.

CRAZY: If you put his brain in a mockingbird, it'd fly backwards. • He's a few straws short of a bale.

CRAZY AS: An outhouse rat.

CRIES, A LOT: She's puttin out more water than an onion chopper in a Cajun restaurant.

CROOKED: As a barrel of fish hooks.

CROSS-EYED: When she cried the tears rolled down her back.

CROWDED: There was more people there than there was at the last white-sock sale down at Wal-Mart.

CUSS HIM: Give him a Confederate talkin' to, which comes from the fact that Confederate soldiers had a penchant for expressing their views with "colorful" language.

CUSSES, A LOT: He could cuss a gate off its hinges.

CUT, SEVERELY: He got more stitches than a patchwork quilt.

CUT IN HALF: In the South you never cut anything in half, you always cut it half in two.

CUTTIN' AND SLASHIN': When mama cuts up a blanket to make daddy a new pair of pants and then cuts up daddy's old pants to make new ones for the children.

 DAMN: Day-um. "Frankly my dear, I don't give a day-um."

DANCER, GOOD: He can dance to the national anthem (or to *Dixie*).

DANCING CLOSE: Where you hold the girl so close you're almost behind her.

DANGEROUS: As a cold Yankee with a chainsaw. A cold Yankee armed with a chainsaw is liable to cut down anything for firewood, including clothesline poles or the only shade tree in the front yard.

DANGEROUS AS: Fire ants in the outhouse.

DANGEROUS SITUATION: That's like trying to milk an alligator, it's fraught with danger at both ends.

DARING: He'd fight a water moccasin with one hand tied behind his back and give the snake three bites head start.

DARK: It's so dark, if you lit one match you'd have to light a second one to see if the first one was burning.

DAUGHTERS, ALL MARRIED: I'm daughtered out.

DAWN TO DUSK: Cain't see to cain't see, which is how long country folks have to work to stay ahead of starvation.

DEAD: As hell in a preacher's parlor or a lightning bug in a cream pitcher.

DEER, LARGE: You could make a rocking chair out of the horns.

DELICATE: As frost on a moonbeam.

DELICIOUS: That's the best I ever wrapped a lip around.

DEMOCRAT, DEVOUT: Yellow dog Democrat, someone who'd vote a Democratic ticket even if a yellow dog was on the ballot.

DEPRESSED: My heart is as heavy as a bucket of hog livers.

DESIRABLE: I'd give up some body parts to get that, which means I want it something fierce.

DESPERATE: You're huntin' hungry. Only a desperate man would go huntin' when he's hungry 'cause it messes up your aim.

DETERMINED: I'm gonna do that even if it harelips every goat in Arkansas.

DIARRHEA: Arkansas two step • Tennessee quick step • The green apple nasties which are brought on by eating green apples or drinking new cider. During the War between the States, Rebels believed that whiskey was a sure cure for Tennessee quick step.

DIED HAPPY: It took the undertaker and his helper three days to get the smile off his face.

DIFFERENCE, DRAMATIC: The only thing they have in common is that neither one of 'em was raised by wolves.

DIFFERENT SITUATION: That's another bucket of possum heads.

DIFFICULT AS: Stretchin' a gnat's butt over a washtub • Sneakin' dawn past a rooster • Shovelin' sunshine.

DIFFICULT SITUATION: There's a lot more alligators than there is rice stalks in that pond. • You're plowin' in sticky mud, which means it'll stick to the blade, making plowing very difficult.

DIFFICULT TO ACCEPT: A hard pill to swallow.

DIMWIT: He has to be watered twice a week. • The only time he knows where he's going is when he takes castor oil.

DINNER CALL: Come and get it before the grease sets.

DIPLOMACY: The ability to dive into a cesspool and not make a splash.

DIPLOMAT: He can tell you to go straight to hell and make you look forward to the trip.

DISADVANTAGE: You're workin' with a short stick, which was said of former Razorback Jimmy Johnson when he became coach of the Dallas Cowboys. (The stick has since grown.) • We weren't playing on a level field. In the 1960 Bluebonnet Bowl, Clemson defeated a much larger TCU team. Following the game, Clemson's Frank Howard explained, "Those other boys were so big they tilted the field and we were able to play downhill all the way."

DISAPPOINTED: As a coyote with a rubber chicken.

DISCOURAGING: As smelling whiskey through a cell door.

DISLIKE HIM, A LOT: I wouldn't wet on him if he was on fire.

DISLIKE IT: Don't cotton to that • Can't sit still for that • That don't sit right by me • I don't hold with that.

DISORIENTED: As a goose in a hailstorm.

DISTANCE: There are varying degrees of distance in the South, as follows: Within spittin' distance is extremely close; if you can chunk a rock and hit it, it's very close; just down the road a piece is close; within hollerin' distance is fairly close; a holler and a half away is farther than fairly close; a see and a half away is starting to get far; a rifle shot away is a fairly long distance; far enough away that you can't hear the dogs is farther still; and a fur piece is a long way.

DISTANCE, MEASURE: For short distances, use the beer method which means the distance is measured by the number of beers that would be consumed in makin' the trip. "It's a three-beer trip from here to Fayetteville." • For longer distances, use the bus change method, which is the number of times you'd have to change buses to get there. "It's a three-change bus trip from Little Rock to Washington, DC but well worth the aggravation."

DISTURBANCE: Somebody hauled hell out of its shuck.

DIVORCED: They separated the dasher from the churn.

DIVORCED, TWICE: He halved his half.

DIXIE (THE PLACE): Arkansas and Tennessee are both part of Dixie, which means they were a part of the Confederacy. The origin of the name "Dixie" is often argued about, but many believe it came from Southerners mispronouncing the French "dix," which was the name for the ten-dollar notes issued by the Banque des Citoyens in New Orleans. *See Section Three*

DIXIE (THE SONG): *See Section Three*

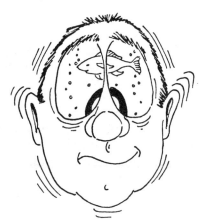

DIZZY: Swimmy-headed. "After a couple of beers, Ethyl gets awful swimmy-headed."

DO IT RIGHT: Hang your wash on a taut line.

DO IT YOURSELF: You gotta milk your own duck.

DO YOUR BEST: Put the best dog you got into the fight.

DOG, GOOD: He's a hard dog to keep under the porch.

DOG, LAZY: His tail only wags when the wind blows it.

DOG, STUPID: He'd get lost chasin' a skunk under the house.

DOG, WORTHLESS: A country store dog. Dogs that hang around country stores don't do much but lay in the sun, eat scraps, and go huntin' with anybody who's going. Such a dog has no loyalty and thus is worthless.

DOG'S NAME: The most common name for a Southern dog is Damn It. "Get in the truck, damn it."

DOING IT WRONG: You're not holding your mouth right, which is often said to someone who is trying to do something but just can't quite get it right.

DOING NOTHING: I'm just sittin' around with my teeth in my mouth.

DOING POORLY: We're livin' off the back forty. The "back forty" is a term used to describe the worst part of a farm, usually heavily wooded with deep ravines and lots of rocks. Anyone living off the back forty would be doin' poorly.

DOING WELL: I got enough shirts and overalls that I don't have to go to bed while mama washes. If you only had one shirt and one pair of overalls you'd have to go to bed while mama washed 'em so you wouldn't be runnin' around the place mostly naked. • We've got goose eggs and new overalls.

DOING VERY WELL: I'm makin' money faster'n a bootlegger in a dry county. In Arkansas, you can legally buy alcohol only in "wet" counties where voters have approved alcohol sales. In dry counties you can always buy it from a bootlegger.

DOLOLLY: Term used to indicate something for which you don't know the name. "When Bubba's truck died he had to replace some dololly under the hood." Synonyms would be dohicky, doodad, thingamajig, dofunny, flung dung, and whatchamacallit.

DON'T FORGET: What you don't have in your head you got in your feet, which means if you forget something, you have to go back and get it.

DON'T KNOW: I have no more idea about that than a sow knows when it's Sunday.

DON'T LIKE: I don't like that and I always will.

DON'T NEED: I need that like a frog needs a face-lift.

DON'T PARTICIPATE: Don't mud wrestle with pigs; all you get is dirty and the pigs love it.

DON'T UNDERSTAND FULLY: I hear the cackling but I can't find the nest.

DOUBLE WIDE: A trailer house created by joining two half trailers. A double wide makes life easier when you get a divorce because you can hook up to your half and drive off.

DOUBTFUL: Pigs'll fly before that happens.

DRAINAGE SYSTEM, ARKANSAS STYLE: Cracks in the floor. If you have enough cracks in the floor, all the rain that comes in through the holes in the roof will drain off.

DREAD: I'd rather skin skunks than do that.

DRESS, SHORT: If she bent over, we could see all the way to Little Rock.

DRESSED UP: He looks like he oughta be deliverin' a sermon or enterin' a plea. • She's wearin' her Sunday-go-to-meeting clothes.

DRESSES, SLOPPY: She looks like her clothes were thrown on with a pitch fork.

DRINK, STRONG: Snakebite serum • Extract of barbed wire.

DRINKER, AVID: He quit drinking when the funnel was invented, which means he now just pours it in.

DRINKER, FEMALE: When she drinks she goes hug wild. • She can level down the cider with the best of 'em.

DRINKER, MALE: If they was selling all the beer you could drink for a dollar, he could drink two dollar's worth. • A two-finger drinker. Up North, two fingers means two fingers next to a one-ounce shot glass to indicate the amount of whiskey in a drink. Down South it can mean two fingers next to a washtub.

DRINKING FROM A GLASS: He's gettin' above his raisin', which is said of anyone in Arkansas who wants to drink out of a glass instead of a jug or Mason jar.

DROPPED: Like yesterday's oats in a horse corral.

DROUGHT: It was so dry we had to spray the catfish for ticks and plow under the hogs.

DRUNK: Commode-hugging, hymn-singing drunk • If he was shot in the head he'd have to sober up to die. • Wobbly-ass drunk.

DRY: As dust in a mummy's pocket • So dry the cows are giving powdered milk.

DUCT TAPE: Arkansas welding rod, so called because it is used to join pieces of metal that should be welded. • Also called "90-mile-an-hour tape" because vehicle repairs made with it are supposedly good till you reach 90 miles per hour.

DUMB: His IQ is about as high as the room temperature. • He couldn't scatter manure with a new $10 rake. • He's about as sharp as a pound of wet liver.

DUMB AS: A barrel of hair.

 EAGER ANTICIPATION: His face is lit up like a new saloon.

EARLY MORNING: Chicken hollerin' time.

EARLY RISER: He has to pry up the sun with a crowbar.

EARS, DIRTY: The only time he washes his ears is when he eats watermelon.

EASY AS: Slidin' off a greased pig backwards.

EASY PART'S OVER: All the white meat is gone.

EASY TO DO: A cake walk. In rural communities, a cake walk is usually held at church socials. The ladies bake cakes and they are arranged on the floor. Then everyone who pays an entry fee starts walking around the cakes. When told to stop, the person next to the designated cake wins it. And they say Baptists don't gamble.

EASY TO USE: As a rocking chair.

EATS A LOT: We had to get the almanac out to see when he would be through eating. • He's eatin' like it's goin' out of style.

EFFECTIVENESS: The more straws in the broom, the more dirt you can move with it.

EFFICIENT: He stacks his wood next to the outhouse. A Southerner knows to stack firewood by the outhouse so his wife can pick up the kindling on her way back in the morning.

EFFORT, WASTED: You can train a jackass all you want, but don't ever look for him in the winner's circle at Hot Springs.

EGG: Arkansas cackle fart • Hen fruit.

EGGS, LARGE: It only takes eight of them to make a dozen.

EGO, DEFLATED: He fell off his high horse.

EGO, LARGE: She thinks she's the only show pig in the pen.
• He's a legend in his own mind.

ELDERLY: He was around when the Dead sea was only sick.

ELECTRICIAN, GOOD: He could rewire a lightning bug so it would blink *Dixie* in Morse code.

EMBARRASSED REPLY: Hush yo' mouth, which is usually said when someone lays an outlandish compliment on you. Bubba: "Ethyl, since you got your teeth fixed an' them warts removed, why you're the prettiest girl in Arkansas." Ethyl: "Bubba, shut yo' mouth. I ain't the prettiest. Cutest, maybe, but not the prettiest." *Note:* Hush yo' mouth is not to be confused with "shut yo' mouth" which is a reply when someone says something controversial or surprising that you don't necessarily want to hear.

EMBELLISHED: He put a little extra straw in the bricks.

EMPLOYEE, BAD: He either don't do what he's told or he don't do anything 'cept what he's told.

EMPLOYEE, GOOD: If he ever leaves, it'll take two men, a mule, and a good dog to replace him.

EMPTY: As a brassiere hanging on a clothesline • As a pickup full of post holes.

EMPTY HEADED: His head is so empty he has to talk with his hands to keep from getting an echo. • You could shoot him in one ear and the bullet would come out the other ear without hitting anything.

ENCROACHMENT: You're pickin' watermelons off my vine.

ENDED ABRUPTLY: He put the quietus on it. Quietus is a favorite Southern word that is used anytime something is halted abruptly. "Bubba put the quietus on the fight when he slapped Billy Fred up side the head with a pool cue."

ENJOYABLE: More fun than playin' in grandma's sheet rows. When grandma hung clean sheets on a clothesline, a row of wet flapping sheets was created that was the perfect place to play until grandma caught ya.

EVACUATED: Like ants pouring out of a burning stump.

EVENTUALLY: By and by. "I'll get that fence fixed by and by."

EVERY MAN FOR HIMSELF: Every man has to skin his own possum.

EVERYTHING: Guts, feathers, beak, cackle and all.

EVIL PERSON: I'd hate to be the preacher who's gonna have to think of somethin' nice to say at his funeral.

EXCEPTIONAL: That beats anything I ever saw or heard tell of.

EXCITABLE: He can raise more of a ruckus than a coyote in a lamb pen.

EXCITED: As a pullet expecting her first egg. • She had to walk sideways to keep from flying.

EXCITING: More fun than fartin' in a flour barrel. • More fun than grandma gettin' her hair caught in the wringer.

EXPECTATIONS, LOW: You can't expect anything from a hog but a grunt.

EXPERIENCE COUNTS: A worn down broom may not look good, but it knows where the dirt is and how to move it.

EXPERIENCED: I've been doin' that since before I shucked my three-corner pants.

EXPLAIN IT BETTER: Wring a little more out of that rag.

EXPRESSION, STRANGE: You look like you're tryin' to pass a peach pit.

EXTRAORDINARY: I'm tellin' you it's somethin' to see.

EXTREMELY: Get out. "That anvil is heavy as all get out."

EYES, BLOODSHOT: They got more red lines than a Mississippi road map.

EYES, CLOSE SET: His eyes are as close together as an earthworm's.

EYES, SOFT: Her eyes look soft as sorghum in a tin plate.

EYES, SUNKEN: Your eyes look like two rabbit pellets in a snowbank.

EYES IN BACK OF HEAD: Very common on Southern women, especially those with children. The standard answer for mama, when asked how she knew something was going on behind her back is, "I've got eyes in the back of my head."

EYESIGHT, GOOD: He can spot a chigger at fifty yards and tell if it's a male or female.

EYESIGHT, POOR: He couldn't see the side of the outhouse if he was sittin' in it.

 FACTS: There are two kinds of facts in the South, plain facts and true facts. Plain facts are ones that are true most of the time but not always. True facts are true facts.

FACTUAL: If it ain't true, the governor of Arkansas is a possum.

FAILURE: His fuse went out before it got to the firecracker.

FAITHFUL: Ya gotta dance with who brung ya.

FALSE: That's as shy of the facts as a goat is of feathers.

FALSE IMPRESSION: Anyone can look tall when surrounded by midgets, as proven by George Bush and Bill Clinton during the 1992 Presidential debates.

FALSE TEETH, GOOD: The best false teeth are those which, when dropped into a spring while getting a drink, can be fished out by tying a chicken bone to a string and dropping it in the water. Really good false teeth will just naturally clamp down on the bone so you can pull 'em up.

FAMILIAR WITH: If his ashes were used for making lye soap, I'd know which bar he was in.

FAMILY: In the South your immediate family is always "the folks." Other relatives are kinfolk. *See also Related, Sort Of*

FAMILY, LARGE: They wore out three storks buildin' that family. • They have enough children to bait a trotline.

FAMISHED: I could eat the south end of a north-bound wormy goat.

FANATIC: Somebody who sticks to his guns, whether they are loaded or not.

FAR AWAY: It's a three-greasin' trip, which means you'd have to grease the wagon three times to get there and back.

FARMER: A butter and egg man who knows everything there is to know about cows, sows, and plows. • Agro American.

FARMER, EXPERT: The only thing he can't do on a farm is lay an egg.

FARMER, LAZY: He don't raise anything but hogs because hogs don't need plowing or hoeing.

FARMER, POOR: He couldn't raise pole beans in a manure pile.

FAST AS: A duck on a June bug • An Arkansas preacher can spot a counterfeit nickel.

FAST PERSON: He can blow out the lamp and get into bed before it gets dark.

FAST WORKER: If he'd been on the Titanic, he could a bailed fast enough to keep her afloat.

FASTER THAN: A three-legged chicken. There was once a man from Arkansas who liked the drumstick when fried chicken was served. The only problem was both of his two sons also liked the drumstick, which meant a fight generally broke out when chicken was served because there were only two legs. To resolve the situation, the man asked the University of Arkansas to breed some three-legged chickens. Six months later, the university delivered six of the unusual birds, but unfortunately the family has yet to enjoy a three-drumstick meal because no one can catch these three-legged chickens.

FAT MAN: If he just had four feet and a snout, he'd qualify for the hog show at the state fair. • He has to stick out an arm to tell if he's walking or rolling.

FAT WOMAN: Her housecoat would fit around a small house. • You can't tell which wrinkle she'll open to talk.

FATE, SEALED: Lightning has struck your outhouse.

FEARLESS: He'd take on a pack of razorback hogs blindfolded.

FEELING BAD: I feel like I was run down, run over, and wrung out through a little bitty wringer.

FEELING GOOD: If I felt any better, I'd have to be twins 'cause one person just couldn't stand it.

FEELING FAIR: I'm still gruntin' but I ain't grinnin' yet.

FEELINGS, HURT: That cut me to the quick. "When Ellie Mae told Bubba he was dumb as a stump it cut him to the quick."

FEET: Dirt movers, which comes from country folks who are always kicking dirt clods while they stand around talking.

FEET, COLD: When he takes off his shoes the furnace comes on.

FEET, LARGE: His feet are so big he has to go down to a crossroad to turn around.

FEET, STINKING: He sits on the front pew in church so he can control the length of the sermon by takin' off his shoes.

FEMALE, ABLE: She can iron all day in high-heel shoes with a cold iron and still go dancing.

FEMALE, AGGRESSIVE: She comes on like a mouthful of hot grits.

FEMALE, ATTRACTIVE: She could make a glass eye blink.

FEMALE, CONFIDENT: She's so confident she can walk past a mirror and not look at it.

FEMALE, CONNIVING: She always smells tired, which means just before her husband gets home she dabs Pine Sol on her neck and sprays Lysol under her arms so she'll smell like she's been working all day.

FEMALE, CRAZY: Her dishes are a few saucers short of a set.

FEMALE, GENTLE: She only hits with the soft end of the mop.

FEMALE, HELPFUL: She'd dip your shirt in catnip if you were going panther hunting.

FEMALE, IGNORANT: She'd have to have an owner's manual to try on shoes.

FEMALE, INEPT: She'd buy cosmetics for a makeup exam.

FEMALE, PROUD: She thinks she's the only peach on the tree.

FEMALE, RESTLESS: A hard gal to keep down on the farm.

FEMALE, SHAPELY: She's built like a brick outhouse, which means nothing sure would look good on her.

FENCE, GOOD: In the South, any fence that is "horse high, pig tight, bull strong, and goose proof" is considered good.

FEVER, HIGH: His forehead was so hot his eyes were almost hard boiled.

FIDDLER, BAD: He plays the fiddle like the strings were still in the cat.

FIDDLER, GOOD: He can make a fiddle sound like a 15-string harp played by a veteran angel.

FIDGETING: Like a three-legged cat tryin' to bury manure on a frozen lake.

FIFTY-GALLON DRUM: One of the most versatile things you can have around the place. You can cut one half in two (end to end) and make an Arkansas Hibachi (BBQ pit) or a matched pair of hog troughs. You can cut one half in two (around the middle) and make a pair of matched planters. You can leave it as is, take the top off, and use it for cooking sour mash or for a trash can. You can weld a whole bunch of 'em together and make a first-rate pontoon boat that'll float real good till the barrels rust out.

FIGHT, BIG: A teeth-gnashing, knockdown, drag-out fight. A really big fight is one where they raised more dust than Noah's flood could have settled. Big fights are said to be the leading cause of death among jukeboxes in Arkansas and Tennessee.

FIGHT, SHORT: A two-hit fight; I hit you, you hit the ground.

FIGHTER, POOR: He couldn't whip a 90-year-old blind, paraplegic grandmother.

FIGHTER, QUICK: He never throws the first punch, he throws the second four.

FINAL ACT: The door slammer, which means the door to further opportunities is closed.

FINANCIAL CONDITION, POOR: I'm like a dog chasin' his tail, we're both tryin' to make ends meet and not gettin' it done.

FINE: As frog hair split three ways.

FINISH THE JOB: Hoe all the way to the end of the row.

FINISHED: You can stick a fork in him 'cause he's done.

FINISHED IT: You put the pin in the party hog.

FIRE ANTS: Imported South American ants that hurt worse than a scorpion, are as tenacious as an angry water moccasin, and are harder to get rid of than a deadbeat brother-in-law.

FIRM BUT FAIR: He's like a watermelon, he's got a big heart but it's hidden under a thick skin.

FIRST THINGS FIRST: The water won't clear up till you get the hogs out of the creek. • A cow can't give milk until after she's had a calf.

FISH, LARGE: A picture of it would weigh five pounds. • You could use the scales for roof shingles. • A wall hanger, which means it's large enough to stuff and hang on a wall. *See also Bass, Large*

FISH, SMALL: You could have it stuffed and used it for a key chain.

FISHERMAN: All are liars except me and you and I ain't so sure about you.

FISHERMAN, AVID: His idea of an anniversary treat is baitin' his wife's hook while they're fishing.

FISHERMAN, CLEVER: He fishes with drunk worms. Clever fishermen dip their worms in whiskey to get 'em drunk so when a fish happens by, the worm will bite it and hold on until you get it in the boat.

FISHERMAN, EXPERT: He has his M.B.A., Master Baiter and Angler, which means he's graduated from the University of Arkansas School of Fish Hook Baiting and Trot-Line Tying.

FISHERMAN, INEPT: He don't know his bass from a hole in the ground.

FISHERMAN, LUCKY: He was born with a silver hook in his mouth.

FISHERMAN'S CREED: It ain't how deep you fish but how you wiggle your worm.

FISHING: The most fun you can have with your clothes on.

FISHING, GOOD: You have to hide behind a tree to put the bait on your hook so the fish won't jump out of the water and grab it out of your hand.

FISHING, POOR: Even the biggest liars weren't catching anything 'cause the fish were biting like tuna in a can.

FISHING LICENSE: Arkansas ID.

FISHING LINE: Arkansas dental floss.

FISHING LURES: Arkansas earrings.

FIST: Arkansas soup spoon • The five of clubs.

FIT, GOOD: Fits like the skin on a snake.

FIT, LOOSE: Fits about as snug as a choir robe.

FIT, POOR: Fits like a sock on a duck's beak.

FLAG, CONFEDERATE: The Stars and Bars.

FLAPPING: Like a runaway window shade.

FLATTERY: Artificial sweetener. John Wayne called it the "phony express." • Sugar mouthing. "Would you just listen to ol' Bubba sugar mouthin' that Sue Ellen."

FLEW APART: Like a $2 suitcase in a bus depot.

FLIGHTY: She's always flyin' up the creek.

FLIMSY: As cheesecloth socks.

FLIRTATIOUS: She can sit on your lap while you're standing up.

FLOOD: There was enough water to float the rock of ages.

FLOOZY: A floozy, in the South, is not necessarily a prostitute. Any painted-up, flirtatious, skin-showing woman with a wiggle in her walk, wickedness on her mind, and whiskey on her breath will be a floozy, according to the fine ladies of the First Baptist Church. A floozy is transformed into a hussy when she steals another woman's boyfriend or husband.

FLOWER PLANTER: In Arkansas (and other parts of the South) the favored flower planter is a used tire. Take any used tire (the more tread left on it, the more you'll impress your neighbors) and paint it white. Fill with a mixture of sand and dirt and plant enough marigolds or petunias to fill up the hole. Garnish with a plastic pink flamingo. The tires make excellent planters because water is trapped inside so the flowers have plenty of moisture. The flamingos, however, rarely grow.

FLY SWATTER: Emergency tea strainer • Fly brush, which is a homemade brush used to shoo the flies off the food.

FOG, THICK: So thick you couldn't cut it with a chainsaw.

FOOD, BAD: Fly repellent, which means even the flies won't eat it. *See Chitlins*

FOOL HEAD: An invisible second head on Southerners that tends to come off easily. "He laughed his fool head off."

FOOLING: You're tryin' to sell me possum hide for rabbit fur.

FOOLISH: He'd jump into the river to get out of the rain.

FOOTBALL SCHEDULE, EASY: They're playin' a Tennessee schedule. In the '20s and '30s the University of Tennessee was notorious for scheduling easy opponents such as the Blind Institute and the Baptist Nurse School. Naturally, Tennessee almost always had a great record, but they didn't necessarily have a great team to match it.

FOOTBALL TEAM, POOR: They had an unbalanced line and the quarterback wasn't even that bright.

FOR A LONG TIME: Till the Devil asks for forgiveness.

FOR SURE: Sure as the world. "I'm gonna get my wife a job next week, sure as the world."

FOREVER: As long as a goose goes barefooted.

FORT LAUDERDALE, FLORIDA: Fort Liquordale.

FOUR-WHEEL-DRIVE VEHICLE: What you'd want to be buried in 'cause there ain't a hole it can't get you out of.

FRACTIOUS: He's got some sand in his gizzard.

FRAGILE: It's only held together by prayer.

FRAIL: He has to be propped up to cuss.

FRAZZLED: A good Southern word with several meanings such as well worn, as in frazzled shirt; messy, your room is sure frazzled; or tense, as in frazzled nerves.

FRECKLES: She looks like she swallowed a quarter and broke out in pennies.

FRIEND: If you have a Southerner for a friend, you'll often hear "As long as I got a biscuit, you got half."

FRIEND, BEST: Somebody that'll lend a hand when you have two broken arms and your nose needs picking.

FRIGHTENED: He was scared witless (or something that rhymes with witless).

FRIGHTENING: Would make the hair on a stuffed possum stand on end.

FRUGAL: He gets out of the bed to turn over to save wear and tear on the sheets.

FRUSTRATED: As a pickpocket in a nudist colony. • As a settin' hen trying to lay a square egg.

FRUSTRATING: As trying to herd cats.

FULL: As an egg is of chicken.

FUN: I'm having more fun than a tick in a blood bank.

FUNERAL FOOD: In the South, when someone dies, it is customary for friends and relatives to gather at the deceased home after the funeral. Naturally, the bereaved family can't be expected to cook, so neighbors and friends pitch in to provide the food. Traditional Southern funeral food includes: Southern fried chicken; baked ham; chicken, grits, or cheese casserole; deviled eggs; iced tea to drink and Jell-O salad for desert.

FUNNY: I laughed so hard I almost popped a gizzard string.

FUTILE: As a bull snake tryin' to make love to a buggy whip.

 GARBAGE DISPOSAL, ARKANSAS STYLE: The back yard.

GARDEN: Generally, in the South, gardens are for vegetables, flower boxes or planters are for flowers. A Southerner is usually so proud of his garden that it's a high insult to refuse an invitation to inspect it. Never, ever, refuse any home-grown vegetables if offered.

GARDEN HOSE: Arkansas teething ring.

GEAR, LOW: Granny gear, so called because in old model cars with standard transmissions, granny almost never got out of low.

GENEALOGY RESEARCH: Hog huntin' in Arkansas.

GENTLE HORSE: He could be used on a merry-go-round.

GET BUSY: Shake the cat out of the quilt. This comes from quilting bees in Arkansas. When a quilt was finished, one young lady would hold each corner and then a cat would be pitched on it. The girls would shake the quilt until the cat ran off and which-ever young lady was closest to the cat when he departed would be the next to marry.

GET IT DONE QUICKLY: Let's get past the house before some ol' cur dog starts barking. This means you want to get something done before someone interferes. "Let's get that tax increase bill past the house before some dog starts barking."

GET OUT: Gather up your shadow and haul it out of here.

GET OUT, QUICKLY: You better cut the anchor chain and row fast enough to boil the water.

GET STARTED: Drive a stake. Almost any buildin' project begins when someone drives a stake to mark the startin' point.

GET TO THE POINT: Go around that pig and get to the tail.

GET TO WORK: Quit spittin' on the handle. • You can't plow a field by turning it over in your mind.

GET UP: Cool the chair, which is a reference to chairs getting warm when you sit in them.

GETTIN MAD: He's cloudin' and fixin' to rain knuckles.

GETTING BEHIND: They're killin' 'em faster'n I can skin 'em.

GETTING OLD: He's feeling his corns more than his oats.

GIVE ME THE FACTS: Give it to me with the hair on.

GLASSES, THICK: His glasses are so thick he looks like he's staring at you through the walls of an aquarium.

GLISTENS: Like hoarfrost in the morning sunshine. Hoarfrost is frozen dew that coats the ground with a thin layer of ice crystals.

GLOWS: Like foxfire at midnight. Foxfire is a fungus that forms in decaying wood and causes a strange, eerie glow at night.

GOING NOWHERE: He's soap-tracked and spinning his wheels.

GOOD DAY: A nekkid-on-the-back-porch kind of day.

GOOD OL' BOY: Any Southern male, between the ages of 18 and 80, who loves his country, his family, his state and who loves to drink, hunt, fish, and raise hell in general. A good ol' boy is a sort of thoroughbred redneck that you'd want on your side in a fight.

GORE, AL: Owl GO'er, the former Senator from the great state of Tennessee who is now Vice President, which means he's government's spare tire. We can only hope that if he's ever needed, he'll be full of air. *See also Vice President*

GOSSIP: About all the Vice President has to do. • Gossip is like slinging fresh manure at a clean white wall. It may not stick but it leaves its mark.

GOT MARRIED: She licked him in. • She got him hitched to a double harness.

GOT RELIGION: He rassled the Devil and won.

GOT THINGS TO DO: I gotta kill a chicken and churn.

GOVERNMENT EMPLOYEE: Somebody who has his snout in the public trough.

GRAB: Grab a holt. "Quick, Bubba, grab a holt of this Evinrude and get it off my foot."

GRANNY-WOMAN (DOCTOR): An elderly lady who is so wise in the use of herbs and home remedies that everybody for miles around comes to her when they're sick. An accomplished granny-doctor could poultice the hump off a camel's back.

GRASS HEIGHT: In the South, grass is measured by how it compares to various animals. Short grass is belly-deep to a worm; medium height grass is tall enough to lose a small dog in; and high grass would be shoulder high on a plow mule.

GRAVY: Dixie butter, so called because Southerners often use gravy in places a lot of other people would use butter, such as on biscuits, bread, mashed potatoes, and grits.

GRAVY, GOOD: Soppin' good, which means you "sop" every drop.

GRAVY, POOR: You couldn't cut it with a Bowie knife.

GRAVY, RED EYE: Gravy made by mixing boiling water and strong black coffee with the juice from fried ham. The gravy is stirred until the liquid is well mixed with the juices and small pieces of ham that were left in the skillet. This delicacy was supposedly named by Andrew Jackson, a real Southern hero, when he remarked that the gravy looked like the "red eyes" of his cook who had gotten very drunk the night before.

GRAVY, THICKENIN': Gravy made by mixing flour and milk into the juice left from cooking meat, usually sausage.

Stir the mixture and cook, usually for quite awhile, until it is good and thick. Another Southern delicacy.

GREED: As they say in the South, "Pigs get fat, hogs get slaughtered."

GREEN BEANS, DRIED: Leather britches. To preserve green beans, Southerners nip off the ends, run a string through them, and hang them up to dry. Once the beans were good and dry they were preserved, more or less. The only problem was when the beans were dry it took a heap a cookin' to bring 'em back to life. The name comes from the fact that when the beans were hung up and dried, they resembled a pair of leather britches hanging on a clothesline.

GREENHORN: He's so green you'd have to tie up one leg to give him a haircut.

GREENS, WILD: Wild greens, often called salit, garden sass, or simply greens, are a staple of the Southern diet, especially among the mountain folks. Common greens are watercress, winter cress, narrow-leaved dock, shepherd's purse, sorrel chickweed, collards, chickweed, henbit, and dandelions.

GREETING: "How's ya' mama and them," which is usually said with sincerity to a close friend. "Them" in this case generally means everyone else in the immediate family. If you want to include other than family members in the greeting, use "how's ya' mama and them and everybody."

GRIN, WIDE: As wide as the wave in a slop bucket.

GRINNING: Like a baked possum. • Like a mule eatin' briars. When a mule eats briars he holds his lips apart, which gives the impression he is, in fact, grinning.

GRIP, STRONG: He's got a grip like a pair of Vise Grips.

GRIP, UNSAFE: A hospital hold, so named because frequently, when you try to do something with an unsafe grip, you wind up in the hospital.

GRITS: Georgia ice cream. Grits are made of dried, ground corn and served with butter and gravy. A staple of the Southern breakfast table. Only Yankees and foreigners would put sugar on their grits in public. Also called "Little Hominy." *See also Hominy*

GROWING FAST: Growin' so fast his shadow can't keep up.

GUARANTEE, ARKANSAS STYLE: If it breaks, you get both pieces.

GULLIBLE: She'd buy a soundtrack album from a silent movie. • He'd buy hair restorer from a bald barber.

GUN, POWERFUL: It'd stop a Plymouth at 100 yards.

 HAD ENOUGH: I've enjoyed about all this I can stand.

HAIR, GREASY: His hair looks like it was combed with buttered toast.

HAIR, MESSY: You look like a chicken that ran through a barbed wire fence backwards.

HAIR RESTORER, GOOD: It'll grow hair on a doorknob.

HAM, CURED: Well-aged, Southern style, honey-cured ham is said to be sweet as a lady's kiss and tender as her love.

HANDLE CAREFULLY: Like you were trying to get a fish hook out of a baby's bottom.

HANDS, LARGE: He could pick the Jolly Green Giant's nose.

HANDS, QUICK: He could steal hubcaps off a moving car.

HANDS, SMALL: When he sticks a finger in his ear, his whole hand goes in.

HANDSHAKE, FIRM: He shakes hands like he's clubbing a snake at a garden party.

HANDWRITING, POOR: Hen scratching. • He can't read his own handwriting when it gets cold.

HANGING ON: Like a tick to Dracula.

HANGING ON, BARELY: Like a rusty muffler on an old pickup.

HANGOVER: My head's hummin' like a ten-penny nail hit by a greasy ball-peen hammer.

HAPPENED QUICKLY: That happened quicker than God can make poor folks in Arkansas.

HAPPY: As a toad frog under a dripping faucet. • As a possum in a cow carcass.

HARD AS: A lightard knot, which is the center of a pine stump that contains a concentration of pine pitch. When fully dried, it takes on the characteristics of a cannon ball.

HARD PART'S OVER: It's time to lick the calf. If you have ever seen a cow giving birth, you know that by the time she gets around to licking the calf, the hard part is over.

HARD SURFACE: So hard a cat couldn't scratch it.

HARD TO DO: As trying to trim the whiskers on the man in the moon. • As flying with water wings.

HARD TO FIND: As bird droppings in a coo-coo clock.

HARD TO SELL: That'd be harder to sell than measles.

HARD WORKER: He could wear out a pair of steel post hole diggers, which are generally thought to be indestructible.

HARDHEADED: You could use his head for a rock crusher.

HAT, TIGHT: I had to stick my head in a boot jack to get it off.

HAVEN'T BEEN THERE: I ain't been within rifle shot of there.

HAVING A BABY: She's gone to the pen.

HEAD, SHAKING: Like a dog killing a snake.

HEADACHE, SEVERE: A diamond splitter. • I'd have to be dead three days before it would stop hurting. • My head's hurtin' so bad, if the two-headed boy in the circus had it he'd have it in both heads.

HEARING, GOOD: He could hear a termite sneeze in the floor of a bowling alley. • He can hear the sun set or the moon rise.

HEARING, IMPAIRED: He couldn't hear a pin drop if it was a cattle pen dropped off a cliff onto a tin-roof barn.

HEART BROKEN: My heart is so broken it's gonna take two quarts of Jack Daniels to splint it. • She broke my heart worse than an egg dropped on a sidewalk.

HEAVY: As a bucket of hog livers. • As a mother-in-law's baggage when she's moving in.

HELL: A Southern measure of extreme, such as hotter'n hell; colder'n hell; crazier'n hell; meaner'n hell; bigger'n hell.

HELL RAISER: He raised more hell than an alligator in a dry riverbed.

HELLACIOUS: A favorite word in the South that can be used for something good or bad that is severe or intense. "They had one hellacious fight down at the Dew Drop Inn last night." • "She gave me one hellacious kiss good-night."

HELPLESS: As a pig in quicksand.

HENPECKED: He's so henpecked he molts twice a year.

HICCUP CURE: The best known cure for hiccups is a turkey shoot for the blind. • The second best known cure for the hiccups is a cross-eyed javelin thrower.

HILLBILLY: A rural person in Arkansas and Tennessee is commonly referred to as a "hillbilly." Synonyms are ridge-runner, gully-jumper, sorghum-lapper, and rabbit-twister. A sophisticated hillbilly is a "hillwilliam." Sophisticated, in this case, is defined as someone who takes the beans out the can before eating them with a knife. Should you actually encounter some of the rural folks, you'd be well advised *not* to use any of the above terms unless you're with a National Guard unit at the time or your insurance is paid up. Folks who live in the mountains prefer "mountain folks" or "mountain people" and anything else is considered derogatory.

HIND LEG: A phrase that baffles Yankees because, on a Southerner, the hind leg is invisible. The phrase means I don't believe you. "The dog drank the beer, my hind leg."

HISSEY FIT: *See Conniption Fit*

HIT HARD: A gizzard loosener, which means you ought to get your breath back in a day or two.

HIT MEDIUM HARD: A stinging lick, which means you'll just have to look out an ear hole to see anything for a couple of hours.

HIT SOFT: Wouldn't bruise a peach.

HOG: Arkansas pine rooter • Acorn chaser. *See also Razorback*

HOLE, SMALL: Peep hole • Spit hole, which is a small hole cut in the wood floor of a cabin to be used as a spittoon.

HOLES, NUMEROUS: That's got more holes than a cabbage leaf after a hailstorm.

HOMESICK: She's wishing she was back under mama's bed playin' with the kittens.

HOMINY: Corn kernels that are boiled until they are three or four times their original size. Sometimes called big hominy. *See also Grits*

HOMINY SNOW: Snow that some believe resembles hominy.

HONEST PERSON: You could shoot dice with him over the phone. • I'd rather have his word than the signature of the President.

HONKY TONK: A Southern bar, usually on the outskirts of town, where the beer is always cold and the women are always willing to dance. In addition to having a jukebox, a honky tonk always has live music at least a few days a week. When you're going out for a night of drinkin', dancin', and fightin' at local honky tonks or juke joints, you are going "jookin'." *See Juke Joint*

HONKY TONK, DANGEROUS: A hold 'em and hit 'em joint where they search you and if you aren't carrying a knife, they rent you one. Some enterprising owners of dangerous honky tonks have found a way to get rich. They charge you $3 dollars to get in and $10 to get out.

HOPELESS SITUATION: You got about as much chance as a pig would have in a dog race.

HOPPING AROUND: Like a migrating bull frog.

HORSE, FAST: He runs so fast he has to keep knockin' the rabbits out of the way.

HORSE, GENTLE: He's as easy to ride as a rocking chair.

HORSE, MEAN: He can buck your whiskers off.

HORSE, STRONG: He's so strong he can carry double and still kick up. This means a horse is so strong that it can carry two riders and still buck.

HORSE, WELL TRAINED: If he jumped off a cliff, you could yell "whoa" three feet from the bottom and he'd stop.

HORSE, WORTHLESS: A jughead, which means he ain't nuthin' but a hay burner.

HORSESHOER, GOOD: He could put iron shoes on a horsefly.

HOT: It was so hot we had to feed the chickens cracked ice to keep them from laying hard-boiled eggs.

HOT ENOUGH: To fry spit, which came from mama spittin' on the iron to see if it was hot. • To boil the water inside a watermelon while it's on the vine.

HOT SPRINGS, ARKANSAS: America's spa, so called because of all the natural hot springs in the area that many believe have healing powers. It was once thought Hot Springs hotels never had to buy firewood 'cause they used the crutches of all the cripples who were cured.

HOUSE, UNKEMPT: An unkempt house in Arkansas is one where you have to use a weed eater inside.

HOUSEKEEPER, INEPT: She boils water to put in her washing machine.

HOW'S THAT AGAIN? Lick that calf again?

HUG: Love their neck, a frequent instruction for Southern children when the grandparents come calling.

HUGGING: They were so twisted up together you couldn't tell where the boy stopped off and the girl commenced.

HUMIDITY, HIGH: I'm sweating setting.

HUMOROUS: That'd make a stuffed owl smile.

HUMPED UP: Like a country girl on an organ stool.

HUNGRY: I got the missed-meal colic. • I'm so hungry if someone laid a biscuit on top of my head, my tongue would slap my brains out.

HUNGRY AS: A woodpecker with a sore pecker.

HUNGRY ENOUGH TO: Eat a plumber's rag. • To eat the stuffing out of a shuck doll.

HUNTER, INEXPERIENCED: He hasn't learned that everything that goes "moo" ain't a moose.

HUNTER, LAZY: The only thing he shoots is the bull.

HUNTING, ILLEGAL: A fire hunter, which means he uses a strong beam of light to "spot" the eyes of deer and other game.

HUNTING DOG, GOOD: He's so good, when a bird flies over he figures out where it'll land when shot, then gets there first so he can catch it in his mouth and keep it from getting dirty. • The truly best hunting dogs are those that'll hunt till you drop.

HUNTING DOG, POOR: He don't know the difference between a possum and a Plymouth.

HURRY: Get high behind like an old rooster in a hailstorm. • Light a shuck, which originated when neighbors often borrowed fire. They'd light a shuck and hurry home 'cause shucks burn fast.

HURT, BAD: My butt and all the fixtures are broke.

HUSSY: *See Floozy*

HYPOCHONDRIAC: He thinks ingrown toenails are catching.

HYSTERECTOMY: Where they get rid of the baby carriage and leave the playpen.

I AGREE: You are preaching to the choir.

I GUESS SO: Hell, I reckon.

I WOULD APPRECIATE IT: I'd take it kindly. "I'd take it kindly if you'd get me a co-cola."

IN AGREEMENT: We're both sittin in the amen corner. • We're chewin' off the same plug.

INBREEDING: The family tree don't have many branches. In some parts of Arkansas the biggest question to ask after a couple gets a divorce is, "Are they still first cousins?"

INDIAN SUMMER: A spell of warm weather that comes after the first frost.

INVITATION, SOUTHERN STYLE: Y'all come. • Come see us. We'll do so many nice things for you you're bound to like some of them.

I DON'T CARE: I don't give a bed bug's behind about that.

I'M NOT LYING: I hope to get kicked to death by a crippled grasshopper if I ain't tellin' the truth.

I'M READY: My hair's set. After a hog is slaughtered it is boiled in hot water, which sets the hair (makes it stands on end) so it can be scraped off easily.

I'VE BEEN THERE: I've been on the pig's side of the pen.

ICE, THIN: Chicken foot ice, which is the first little layer of ice that forms on a pond. The ice has small crack-like imperfections which resemble chicken feet.

IDIOT: You could keep him busy for half a day by asking him to find the top of a ball bearing. • If the power failed, he could get trapped on an escalator.

IDLE: He's as busy as a telephone operator in a ghost town.

IF: If a pig had wings, he'd be a chicken hawk.

IGNORANT: He'd play Russian roulette with a single-shot rifle. • He'd have to study up to be a half-wit.

IGNORE HIM: Just play like his mother didn't have any children that lived.

ILL: He's down with the miseries.

ILL, GRAVELY: It's time to get the chickens out of the hearse.

ILLEGAL: On the hot side of the law.

ILLEGITIMATE: He's a descendent of a long line his mother heard in a juke joint.

ILLITERATE: He signs his name with a holler 'cause he can't even make an X.

IMMATURE: He oughta be home playing with a string of spools.

IMPOSSIBLE: You can't sweep sunshine off the porch. • You can't keep dew off the grass. • In a turkey's dream you can.

IMPOTENT: He's ain't got no lead in his pencil. • His Evinrude won't crank.

IMPRACTICAL: Makes as much sense as an artificial wart.

IMPRESSION, FALSE: Just 'cause a hog has hair don't mean he can grow sideburns.

IMPRESSION, STRONG: That made more of an impression than a three-legged man in a butt kicking contest.

IMPRESSIONABLE: Her head is like a doorknob, anyone can turn it.

IN A QUANDARY: I'm up against a stump.

IN DISARRAY: Everything's all boogered up.

IN ERROR: That's a bull you're tryin' to milk.

IN EVERY DIRECTION: Everwhichaways. • Seven ways from Sunday.

IN PAIN: I feel like a parakeet that got caught in a badminton game.

IN POOR CONDITION: It'll take a faith healer to repair it.

IN TROUBLE: The slop has hit the fan. • We're in a bad row of stumps.

INCLINED: Got a mind to. "I've got a mind to whup your butt."

INCLINED, SOMEWHAT: Got half a mind to. "I've got half a mind to paint the barn."

INCOMPETENT: He couldn't be the crew chief on a sunken submarine.

INCOMPLETE: As a kiss without a squeeze.

INCONSEQUENTIAL: As a bee sting to a honey lovin' bear.

INDECISIVE: He does a great imitation of a weather vane.

INDEPENDENT: As a hog on ice.

INDIVIDUALISM: Every pot has to stand on its own bottom.

INDUSTRIOUS: His kindling box is always full.

INEFFECTIVE: As a pint of whiskey split five ways.

INEFFICIENT ORGANIZATION: We got too many colonels and not enough infantry.

INEPT: In a battle of wits, he'd be an unarmed man.

INEVITABLE: Sooner or later, every chimney smells of smoke.

INEXPERIENCED: There are only three things he can do and all of them are nothing.

INFATUATED: He's got his hat set for her.

INFLATION PRESSURE: When the price of syrup goes to a dollar a sop, the biscuit stays mighty dry.

INFURIATED: He was spouting steam from every joint.

INGENIOUS: He could split something down the middle and still get the biggest half.

INNOCENT: As a fresh laid egg.

INSANE: If you were gonna drive him crazy, it'd be a short trip.

INSIGNIFICANT: It ain't nuthin' a man on a gallopin' horse would notice. • During his ill-fated 1992 presidential campaign, H. Ross Perot, who grew up five blocks from Arkansas, defined insignificant as "one mosquito at a picnic for ten thousand people."

INSIGNIFICANT PERSON: He's just a little frog in a big pond.

INSINCERITY: He's like chicken droppings, warm when they come out of the chicken and cold when they hit the ground.

INSOMNIAC: He gets less sleep than a man with three daughters and two back doors.

INSULT: If you were mine, I'd trade you for a flea-bitten, mangy old hound dog and then shoot the dog.

INTELLECTUAL: In Arkansas and Tennessee, the way they know someone is an intellectual is if he can listen to the *William Tell Overture* and *not* think of the Lone Ranger. A true Arkansas intellect can also explain how a Thermos bottle knows to keep coffee hot and cold drinks cold.

INTELLIGENCE, AVERAGE: He wasn't in the top half of his class but he was one that made the top half possible.

INTELLIGENT: He's so smart he'll have to forget something before he can learn anything new.

INTERFERING: You're hanging your wash on my line.

INTERRUPTION REPLY: Who mashed your button?

INVOLVED: I got some hogs in those bottoms, which refers to everyone letting their hogs run free in the bottoms and then everyone shares in the meat.

INVOLVED DEEPLY: He went whole hog.

IRRESISTIBLE: As rabbit liver is to a catfish.

IRREVOCABLE: Once you make a steer, you can't turn him back into a bull.

IS THAT RIGHT: Sure enough? Primarily used as a reply when somebody tells you something that's hard to believe.

ISN'T THAT SOMETHING: Ain't that the berries.

IT'S OVER: You might as well call in the dogs and wet on the fire.

J

JACK DANIELS: Black Jack; smooth sippin' Tennessee whiskey.

JEALOUSY: He wouldn't trust her if she had a date with the Pope. • The only time she trusts him is when he's in sight.

JEANS, TIGHT: Her jeans were so tight, I could hardly breathe. • Swift and Company never packed a ham in a can as tight as her butt is packed in them jeans.

JILTED: Her bass spit out the hook.

JOB: Something for people who don't fish.

JOB, BIG: I lacked one hand of being able to do it, which means it was more than a one-man job.

JOB, UNFINISHED: You still got some creeks to cross. • You still got some syrup to sop.

JOB, UNPLEASANT: If you have to drink from a spittoon, do it in one quick gulp.

JOHNNYCAKE: Cornmeal cake made from a mixture of meal and water that is baked until brown and crispy.

JOIN IN: A dog enjoys the hunt a lot more if he does some of the barkin'.

JOKE, OLD: The first time I heard that I was serving detention in the first grade.

JUDGMENT: Judge a man by the taste of his pork, not how the pig squealed. • Judge a woman by how her biscuits taste, not how they look.

JUDGMENT, POOR: You're selling horses to buy horse feed.

JUKE JOINT: A Southern bar which resembles a honky tonk except there is no live music, only a jukebox. A true Southern juke joint must have a pool table or two. *See also Honky Tonk*

JUMPED: Like he'd just stepped on the sun.

JUMPED ON, QUICK: He jumped on me so quick I thought I was under a bridge that had collapsed.

 KEEP ACTIVE: Flies don't come around a boilin' pot.

KEEP BUSY: Tend to your knitting.

KEEP THE FAITH: Keep your dauber up and your dander down.

KEEP TRYING: It's OK to give out but don't never give in.

KEEP WORKING: Keep the sifter going, which means keep working so you can buy enough flour to sift for biscuits.

KEEP YOUR MOUTH SHUT: I don't want to hear a peep outa you, a favorite saying of Southern mothers.

KETTLE, LARGE: Wash-pot, which is used for just about everything in Arkansas from washing (boiling) clothes, to making lye soap, to giving the small kids their Saturday bath.

KID: Southerners frequently add "of a boy." I was just a kid of a boy when I started chewing tobacco and sippin' whiskey."

KIDDING: He's wettin' in my boots and telling me it's raining.

KIND: He wouldn't hurt a chigger.

KIND BUT DUMB: He's whole hearted but half-witted.

KIND HEARTED: She'd buy crutches for a lame duck.

KISS: Sugar • Swap slobber. "Quick, get me the mouthwash 'cause the dog just swapped slobber with me." • A kiss is a mouth full of nothing that sounds like an old milk cow pulling her foot out of a mud bog. • Remember, kissing don't last but cooking does.

KISS, QUICK: *See Yankee Dime*

KNIFE: Arkansas silverware setting. There isn't anything in Arkansas that can't be eaten with a knife except soup.

KNIFE, DULL: This knife's been to breakfast, which means it was dulled cutting the food. • That blade is so dull you could ride to town on it and not get cut.

KNIFE, LARGE: Arkansas toothpick.

KNIFE, POCKET TYPE: Apple peeler.

KNIFE, SHARP: The shadow of the blade could cut off a table leg.

KNIFE FIGHT VICTIM: He's been stabbed so many times you could stick a garden hose down his throat and use him for a lawn sprinkler.

KNOCKED DOWN: He went down like a still in a cyclone.

KNOT, TIGHT: A Case knot, which is one that is tied so tight you have to use a Case knife and cut the rope to get it undone. Generally, a Case knot is tied by someone (a Yankee, perhaps) who doesn't know how to tie a tight knot properly so it can be undone without ruining the rope.

KNOW YOUR WORTH: Every ol' sausage knows if he was made from a hog or a dog.

KNOWLEDGEABLE: He knows more about it than a whiteface calf knows about sucking.

LABORING: Like an idiot with a short pencil.

LADIES MAN: He's sowed more wild oats than all the farmers in Kansas combined.

LAND, DRY: So dry we had to put on postage stamps with paper clips. • It takes twenty years for a nail to rust.

LAND, FERTILE: You could plant some wind and grow a windmill. • You can plant a feather and grow a pillow.

LAND, POOR: You'd have to put fertilizer around the bottom of a pole to raise a flag. • You couldn't raise an umbrella on it.

LAND, RICH: As the dirt in a cow pen. • This land is so rich we can't ship crops 'cause the seeds refuse to leave.

LAND, STEEP: We could look up the chimney and watch the cows come home. • You could fall off your corn field.

LARGE AMOUNT: Got more of those than there are liars in Washington, DC. • More than you can shake a stick at.

LARGE BABY: Porch baby, which is one that isn't walking, but you can let it crawl around the porch while you're shelling peas.

LARGE MAN: He was born on the 8th, 9th, and 10th of September. • You think he never will get through gettin' up. • He has to curl up to lay down in a boxcar.

LARGE WOMAN: She's well watered. • She fell down and rocked herself to sleep trying to get up.

LAST CHANCE: If you don't win this time, the giant sucking sound you hear will be your chances going down the drain, to paraphrase Ross Perot.

LAST PLACE FINISHER: He got the pig's tail. When country folks slaughter a pig they use virtually every part except the tail and the squeal, so if all you got was the tail, you lose.

LASTS FOREVER: That lasts as long as an ex-husband.

LAUGH HARD: Enough to shake a tonsil loose from its roots.

LAWSUIT: Something you go into as a hog and come out of as sausage.

LAWYER: As they say in the South, the only difference between a dead lawyer and a dead possum laying on the road is skid marks in front of the possum.

LAWYER, POOR: Hiring him to settle your problem would be like hiring General William Tecumseh Sherman to hold a barbecue in Atlanta.

LAZY MAN: If his house caught fire, he'd start praying for rain. • He'd walk into a river so he could get a drink without having to bend over. • He'd stop plowin' to fart. • He wouldn't hit a lick at a snake.

LAZY WOMAN: She's so lazy she don't even shave her legs. She just spreads cream on 'em and lets the cats lick it off. • The only exercise she gets is jumping to conclusions.

LEADER: The bell cow. *See also Boss*

LEADER, INEPT: If he lined up a firing squad, he'd arrange them in a circle.

LEADER, POOR: Leadership ain't a snug fit on him.

LEAKS: Like a bottomless bucket.

LEAVE: Why don't you run around the barn three times and come back twice. • Skeedadle out a here.

LEAVE ME ALONE: Don't crank my motor unless you want to see it runnin'.

LEAVING: I'm off like a prom dress. • I'm off like a Roman candle. • Gonna haul my sorry butt out a here.

LEE, GENERAL ROBERT E. Gen'rl Lee, the most hallowed of Southern heroes.

LEERY: This old crow has eaten enough field corn to know scarecrows sometimes carry shotguns.

LEFT IN A HURRY: She took off like a chicken through a hole in the fence.

LEGS, SHAPELY: She's got legs like a Tennessee Walking Horse.

LEGS, THIN: You ought to sue those legs for nonsupport.

LEMONADE, SOUR: That would even make the pitcher pucker.

LENGTH, EXAGGERATED: It was measured using a coon skin with the tail on.

LET ME DO IT: It's my turn to rock that baby.

LET'S DISCUSS THAT: Let's pluck that chicken.

LEVEL HEADED: He's so level headed tobacco juice runs out of both sides of his mouth.

LIAR, FEMALE: She has to send the dog for the kids 'cause they won't come when she calls 'em.

LIAR, MALE: He never lets the truth stand in the way of a good story. • He has to hire someone to call in his dogs.

LIBERAL, VERY: He's such a liberal he says "chigro" instead of chigger.

LICK LOG: A lick log is a fallen tree with several notches cut along the top side. Salt is poured into the slots so cattle can lick it out. The lick log has always been a part of the Southern language and that trend may continue with Bill Clinton in the White House. He used the phrase "down to the lick log" the meaning of which, according to *Newsweek* magazine, wasn't even clear to his staff. Clinton used the phrase to indicate when things go to the finish line, which would translate into cattle having finished eating their feed and getting down to the lick log. More common "lick log" uses would be: Interfering. "Your cows are on my lick log." • Joined. "He came over to our lick log." • In agreement. "We're all lickin' off the same log."

LIE: That's as shy of the truth as a possum is of gold teeth. • There are three kinds of lies: lies, damn lies, and Chamber of Commerce statistics.

LIFETIME: All my born days. "I've been a Rebel all my born days."

LIGHT: As a mother-in-law's baggage when she's moving out.

LIGHTER WOOD: Kindling, generally pine wood that is so dry it catches on fire so quickly you think it exploded.

LIKE FATHER, LIKE SON: Fruit don't fall far from the tree.

LIKELY: He's bad to do it. "Jim Bob is bad to miss work when the fish are even close to bitin'."

LIKELY TO: Libel to. "If your wife catches you drinkin' she's libel to snatch you bald-headed."

LIMITED CAPABILITIES: His pony only knows one trick.

LIMP: As a worn out fiddle string.

LIPS, ATTRACTIVE: Her lips are like a large gash in a big juicy peach.

LISTEN TO ME: Let me tell you what.

LITTLE ROCK: The capital of the great state of Arkansas • Arkansas wedding ring.

LIVELY: As a coyote with a knot in his tail.

LIVESTOCK, LACKING: I ain't even got a scapegoat.

LIVING ABOVE YOUR MEANS: Eatin' ham on sowbelly wages.

LIVING DANGEROUSLY: Messin' with your heartbeat.

LIVING SUMPTUOUSLY: He's livin' high off the hog • He's steppin' in high cotton.

LOCATED NEARBY: It's in this neck of the woods.

LOCATION, GOOD: This ain't heaven but you can see heaven from here, which Southerners frequently say about their state.

LONESOME: As a preacher on payday.

LONG: As a country mile. • As a Georgia well rope.

LONG AGO: Before the frost melted off hell. • When snakes walked. • When Moby Dick was just a minnow.

LONG LASTING: As a crowbar. • As an ex-wife.

LONG TIME: A month a Sundays. • A coon's age.

LONG TIME BETWEEN KISSES: The great Minnie Pearl may have said it best with, "I haven't been kissed in so long I didn't remember if you suck in your breath or let it out."

LONG WINDED: He goes all the way 'round the barn to make a point.

LOOK, MEAN: She looked like my dog just ate her best hen.

LOOK, SWEET: So sweet you could pour it on a biscuit.

LOOKING FOR TROUBLE: He's scratchin' around in the turmoil pen.

LOOKS LIKE: Favors • He's a pieprint of his daddy • They're the spittin' image of each other.

LOOKS SICK: You're lookin' a little green around the gills.

LOOSE: As a goose. • As a busted egg.

LOSER: He grabbed the wrong end of the poker.

LOSING: You're paying the wrong preacher.

LOSING WEIGHT: He looks like he's evaporating.

LOSS, LARGE: That left a big hole in the hedge, frequently said of a good person who dies.

LOST: As an outhouse in fog. • Couldn't find hide nor hair of it.

LOST CONTROL: Flew off the handle. • Went hog wild.

LOST HIS APPETITE: He's off his feed.

LOST PERSON: He was so lost he had to run an ad in the paper for someone to come and get him.

LOST UNEXPECTEDLY: We got snuck up on.

LOUD MOUTH: His bark is enough, he don't need a bite.

LOVE: Is like the morning dew, just as apt to be on chicken droppings as on a marigold bloom.

LOVESICK: He'd wash her feet and drink the water.

LOW: As a frog in a post hole.

LOW-DOWN PERSON: He is so low-down he can walk under a trundle bed and not knock off his hat.

LUCKY: He could fall into the squat hole in an outhouse and come out smelling like a Hot Springs floozy.

LUKEWARM: Country cold. Country boys frequently buy a six-pack of beer that they expect to drink right away so they don't bother to buy ice. If there's only one drinking, the last beer will be lukewarm (country cold) but still highly drinkable.

LYE SOAP: A potent homemade soap made from lard and lye that is excellent for washing kids, clothes, and chicken droppings off the porch. It'll also wash off your hide if used before properly cured.

MAH: Possessive form of Ah (I). "When ah fell down ah landed on mah new hat an' ruint it."

MAILBOX: Arkansas clothesline pole.

MAKE A CHOICE: You can't sell your chickens and keep the feathers.

MAKE IT BETTER: Put a little spit on that apple.

MAKE IT EASIER: Put the hay down where the goats can get it.

MAKE IT SHORT: Knock some links out of that chain.

MAKE PEACE: Bury the hatchet.

MAKE PEACE, SORT OF: Bury the hatchet but leave the handle sticking out.

MAMA'S BOY: He's such a mama's boy that he cried when the doctor cut the cord.

MAN: A man is like a watermelon, you can't tell how good he is until you thump him. • Most men are like barbed wire, they have their points.

MAN, ANGRY: He's fightin' with his hat, which means he has taken off his hat and is swingin' it everwhichway. Generally speaking, when a country boy starts fighting with his hat, it's a prelude to fighting with fists or firearms.

MAN, EFFEMINATE: He's got a little sugar in his blood.

MAN, EVIL: There ain't nothing wrong with him that a good cremation wouldn't cure.

MAN, SHORT: He always looks like he's standing in a hole.

MAN, TOUGH: He's the toughest man west of any place east.

MANNERS, POOR: He'll wait on you like one hog waits on another.

MANNERS, GOOD: *See Section Three*

MARKSMANSHIP, GOOD: He shoots seein' eye bullets. • He could shoot off a mosquito's manhood at 50 yards.

MARKSMANSHIP, POOR: He couldn't hit the side of an outhouse if he fired from inside it.

MARRIED, OFTEN: She's been married so many times she has rice scars.

MARRIED, WELL: He didn't pick up a crooked stick, which is usually said of a man who marries a good woman.

MASON-DIXON LINE: The dividing line between youse guys and y'all.

MASS CONFUSION: Three truckloads of bean pickers and no foreman.

MATCHES: Arkansas air freshener.

MATTRESS: Arkansas ironing board, which refers to putting clothes between mattresses to "smooth" out the wrinkles.

MEAN AND STUPID: He'd take a knife to a gunfight.

MEAN AS: An Alabama wildcat with a toothache.

MEAN CHILD: He's so mean, his mama gives him a bath by carrying him down to the creek and beating him on a rock. • Her mother had to feed her with a slingshot, she was so mean.

MEAN MAN: He'd steal acorns from a blind sow and then kick her for squealing. • He'd put a barbed wire fence around a kindergarten.

MEAN WOMAN: If she died, everyone would rest in peace. • She'd dip your shorts in catnip and then buy a mountain lion for a pet.

MEANINGLESS: As earrings on a hog. • As a striptease to a blind man.

MEASUREMENT, APPROXIMATE: Some Southerners use an ax handle as an approximate unit of measure. "Her butt's about two ax handles wide."

MECHANIC, POOR: He's called "waitin' for parts" because that's all he ever seems to be doing.

MEDICINE, POOR: That medicine was so bad I was sick for three weeks after I got well.

MEDICINE, QUICK ACTING: Goes through you like corn through a goose.

MEET A CHALLENGE: Take the bull by the tail and face the situation.

MEMORY, POOR: He could hide his own Easter eggs.

MENTALLY OFF: He acts like he's got a brain cramp.

MESSED UP, SEVERELY: That's so messed up it'd make a wood rat eat cheese.

MILK COW, POOR: A coffee cow, which is one that barely gives enough milk to put in the coffee.

MIND YOUR OWN BUSINESS: Tend to your own bees. • Keep your snout out of my trough.

MISER: He's still got half of his third grade allowance.

MISERABLE: I've got so much misery, if I was triplets all three of us would be miserable.

MISTAKE: Anyone can make a mistake, but it's always somebody else who makes the damn fool mistakes.

MISTAKEN: Your calf ain't sucking the right cow.

MISUNDERSTOOD: I think I opened the hymnal to the wrong page.

MIXED EMOTIONS: When your daughter comes home from the prom carrying a Bible from the Gideons. • "Paddlefoot" Sloan, an Arkansas Razorback back in the 1930s, said he had mixed emotions about the University of Arkansas leaving the Southwest Conference and becoming a member of the Southeastern Conference. "It's like your mother-in-law driving off a cliff," he said, "in your Cadillac."

MODEST: She makes her husband wear a blindfold when they shower together. He can't even tell the naked truth.

MONEY: The mother's milk of politics.

MONEY CLIP, ARKANSAS STYLE: Paper clip.

MOOCHER: He's always got a mouthful of grin and a handful of thank you, which means he's always borrowing something (lawnmower, chainsaw, etc.) but never offers to pay, and if he happens to bring it back, it won't be clean and may not be running.

MOON PIE: The most popular sweet in the South and they're not even real pies. A Moon pie is three cake-like round cookies separated by a marshmallow filling and dipped in chocolate. When eating a Moon pie, the preferred drink is R.C. Cola, usually pronounced R.O.C. Cocola.

MOONSHINE: Only visitors call it moonshine. It's usually shine or cat, which is short for wildcat whiskey. It's also called white lightnin', corn squeezin's, Tennessee tea, mountain dew, worm medicine, O-be-Joyful or any of a number of other names.

MOONSHINE, BAD: Whether it's called panther spit, witch's piss, embalming fluid, or anything else, it always tastes like it came out of a jackass with a kidney problem.

MOONSHINE, GOOD: You can taste the sweat of the farmhand that hoed the corn it was made from.

MOONSHINE, JUST RIGHT: If it was any worse I wouldn't a drunk it, and if it was any better you wouldn'a given it to me.

MOONSHINE, SMOOTH: It's smooth as a moonbeam.

MOONSHINE, STRONG: It goes four or five fights per jug.
• Would cause a frog to spit in a whale's eye.

MOONSHINE, WEAK: It has all the kick of a 95-year-old arthritic chorus girl.

MOONSHINE DRINKER, DEVOUT: It is easy to spot an avid moonshine drinker; he'll have a permanent indention on his nose caused by pressing the lip of a Mason jar against it over a prolonged period of time.

MOONSHINE TEST: To determine if moonshine is good for you or not, do the following test. 1. Get two glasses and fill one with water and one with moonshine. 2. Drop a worm into the glass of water and observe that the worm lives. 3. Drop a worm into the glass of moonshine and observe that he dies quickly. Conclusion: If you drink moonshine, you won't have worms.

MOSQUITO, LARGE: Big enough to stand flat footed on the ground and kiss a rooster on the beak.

MOUNTAIN OYSTERS: Testicles that are removed from a calf during castration and then deep fried. Considered a delicacy in many parts of the South. Testicles from turkeys, pigs, and lambs can also used.

MOUTH, DRY: Feels like the Yankee army marched through my mouth in their sock feet.

MOUTH, LARGE: He's got a mouth big as a grader blade. • Her mouth is so large she gets lipstick on her ears when she smiles.

MOUTH, THE MORNING AFTER: My mouth feels like a buzzard roosted in it all night.

MOVING AROUND: Like a huckleberry in a wagon bed.

MUCH LESS: Let alone. "I can't afford the pickup, let alone the insurance."

MUD SLEEPING SICKNESS: A disease that strikes Arkansas pigs who spend a lot of time in the mud. A mud ball forms on a pig's tail and then grows as he moves around. Eventually, the ball gets so heavy it causes the pig's skin to draw up so tight he can't close his eyes and he dies from lack of sleep.

MUDDY ENOUGH: To bog a bird's shadow.

MULE, ARKANSAS STYLE: A mule whose legs are six inches shorter on the right side so he remains level while plowing a field in Arkansas. An Arkansas mule works great when plowing, but when you get to the end of the field, you have to back him down the mountain. Arkansas mules are also noted for being rather small, so much so that if one happens to drift into Texas, he's usually shot for a jackrabbit.

MUMBLETY-PEG: A Southern game played with a knife, usually outdoors unless it's raining. The first player throws the knife in some fancy way and if it sticks, the other player must throw the knife in the same manner. The game continues until one of the players thinks of something better to do. It has been rumored that Bill Clinton will use the game of mumblety-peg, played with very large knives, to solve international disputes.

MUSIC, GOOD: Foot stompin' music, which means it's so good you can't help but pat your foot.

MUSIC LOVER: If he hears a pretty girl singing in the bathtub, he puts his ear to the keyhole.

MUSICIAN, GOOD: He could play a shoe if you tied the strings tight enough.

MUSICIAN, POOR: The proper pitch for his guitar would be out the window.

 N: And. Southern folks rarely take time to say "and." Generally the "a" and the "d" are discarded and only the "n" is left. "We're gonna have coon 'n collards for supper." • Than. Southerners also frequently use "n" in place of than. "It was hotter'n hell today."

NAIVE: He could be held up through the mail. • She'd play Go Fish with a mind reader.

NAKED AS: A scalded hog, which refers to the hair being scraped off a scalded hog leaving it naked.

NAME, UNKNOWN: *See Dololly*

NARROW MINDED: He's so narrow minded his ears rub together.

NATIVE: In the South, you are not "a native of," you are a native born. "Bill Clinton is a native born Arkansawer."

NAVEL: Where the Yankee shot you.

NEARLY: Nearbout. "It's nearbout ten miles to town." • Nigh. "He ain't got nigh as much cash since he went to Hot Sprangs."

NEARSIGHTED: He can't tell toothpaste from Preparation H.

NECESSARY: You don't get lard unless you boil the hog.

NECK, LARGE: If you put him into a guillotine, it'd take three chops to cut off his head.

NECKTIE: Arkansas funeral tie, which means a lot of folks in Arkansas only wear a tie when attending a funeral.

NEEDS ATTENTION: That ol' hog needs sloppin'.

NERVE: He's got more nerve than an abscess in an elephant's tusk.

NERVOUS: She's shaking so much she could thread the needle on a sewing machine with it a running.

NERVOUS AS: A long tailed cat in a rocking chair factory.

NERVY: He's got more nerve than a pickpocket at a sheriff's convention.

NEVER DO IT, HER: Never learn to change a tire; you'll be expected to do it.

NEVER DO IT, HIM: Never learn to iron; someone will expect you to do it.

NEVER ENDING: That's like wiping with a bicycle inner tube; you never come to the end.

NEVER MARRIED: She always drove her ducks to the wrong market.

NEW DEVELOPMENT: That's a new wrinkle in the quilt.

NO HURRY: Get it done by the second Wednesday of next week.

NO INTENTION: Not about to. "I'm not about to loan you my new pickup."

NO MATTER WHAT: Come hell or high water.

NO SIMILARITIES: They're no more alike than nylon hose and a garden hose.

NO SUCH THING: There ain't no such thing as betting too much on a winning horse or being a little pregnant.

NO WORK, NO PAY: Them that don't pluck, don't get no feathers. This saying comes from plucking geese to get feathers for mattresses and pillows. Usually, if you didn't do your share of the plucking, you slept on the ground.

NO: Southerners hardly ever use just a "no" to answer a question in the negative. Instead, they reply with a question, the answer for which is an obvious no. "Does a chicken have lips?" • "Can a rattlesnake whistle *Dixie?*"

NOISE, LOUD: It jarred everything off the ground. • Loud enough to wake the dead. • You couldn't hear yourself think.

NOISE, OMINOUS: As a gunshot in a graveyard.

NOISY: As a chicken coop full of fifty chickens and one fox.

NOISY EATER: Sounds like a pig eatin' charcoal.

NONE (MONEY): Penny one. "Bubba said he'd pay me twenty-five dollars for them possum hides, but I ain't seen penny one."

NONEXISTENT: As mare's eggs or bull's milk.

NOSE, LONG: They always picked him to play Pinocchio in the school play.

NOT ALL THERE: He's a few dominos short of a set.

NOT FUNNY: That's about as funny as a constipated chicken.

NOT INTERESTED: I don't give a hoot or a holler.

NOT INVOLVED: I don't have a dog in that fight.

NOT MOTIVATED: He's like a wheelbarrow; he stands still until someone pushes him.

NOT NEEDED: I need that about as much as a cow needs a fifth teat.

NOT PRACTICAL: You can shear a pig but you'll get a lot more noise than wool.

NOT TOO BRIGHT: He don't know nuthin' and he's got that all screwed up.

NOTHING IS IMPOSSIBLE: Any cow can eat a salt block if she does it one lick at a time.

NOTHING REALIZED: I got what the bear grabbed at and missed.

NOTHING TO DO: He's got about as much to do as Vice President Al Gore. All he has to do is call the White House every morning and ask, "How's the President feeling?"

NUISANCE: He's a pain in the back of the lap.

NUMEROUS: As cannonballs at Gettysburg.

OAF: He could make a pitchfork complicated.

OATH: I hope your mother crawls out from under the porch and bites you, which is a subtle Southern way of calling someone an S.O.B.

OBLIGATED: If you give a dance, you gotta pay the fiddler.

OBLIGED: I'm not one to thump a free melon. To determine if a melon is ripe, you thump it and judge the sound. When given a free melon you would be obliged to accept it without thumping.

OBSERVANT: He could spot a mole on a hoochiecoochie dancer from fifty feet in a smoke-filled room.

OBSTINATE: If he don't like where you got it, he'll tell you where to put it.

OBVIOUS: Plain as day. "I saw Bubba hit him plain as day."

OCCASIONALLY: Ever once in a while.

OCCURRENCE, RARE: Happens every once in a blue moon.

ODD: That's a chicken of a different color.

ODDS, POOR: The chances of that happening are about the same as you driving off a bridge and stopping before you hit water.

ODOR, BAD: I've been around stills that smelled better than that. The main reason stills are located way out in the woods is that the process of turnin' corn into whiskey is a smelly affair. • That smells worse than Wildroot Cream Oil.

ODOR, GOOD: Smells good as a teenager waiting for her first date.

OF COURSE: W'y yea-us, which is a traditional Southern reply when the answer is obviously "of course." For an emphatic "of course" reply use "hail yea-us" or "damn straight."

OFFICE, LARGE: If we could figure out how to freeze the floor we could skate on it.

OFFICE, SMALL: If you hung a fish on the wall, it'd have to be a sardine.

OKRA: Sometimes called okree. When dipped in batter and fried, okra becomes "The Pod of the Gods" in the South.

OLD: As the Ozarks, which are believed to be several million years older than the Rockies.

OLD PERSON: He's been around since Sitting Bull was a calf. • She was already old when Little Rock was just a platt. In the South, old-timers are considered a "blessing" by their relatives. "Uncle Glen is such a blessing, I just love to hear his stories." Some old folks who are still very active will often say, "I ain't ready to be a blessing yet."

ON YOUR OWN: It's root hog, or die.

ONE OF A KIND PERSON: He was delivered by an eagle instead of a stork.

ONE OR THE OTHER: One. "You gotta fish or cut bait, one."

ONE-HOLER: An outhouse with seating room for one person at a time. It naturally follows that a two-holer and a three-holer would have seating room for two and three persons respectively, although three-holers are extremely rare. According to an old country legend, if you want to confuse someone from Arkansas, just send him into a two-holer. As the story goes he'll mess up his shorts before he can decide which hole to use. When using an outhouse, always knock before entering, beware of spiders, and never remove the Sears catalog no matter how bad you want to order something.

A Primer on Arkansas and Tennessee Words and Ways

ONE-SIDED: As a turkey shoot.

ONE-TIMER: He's a sparkler, which means he'll burn bright for a minute or two, then go out.

OPEN A WINDOW, SLIGHTLY: Crack the window.

OPINIONS: Are like navels, everybody has one.

OPOSSUM: *See Possum*

OPPONENT, EASY: A breather. Every football coach likes to have one or two breathers on his schedule every year. *See also Football Schedule, Easy*

OPPORTUNITIES, LACKING: The pickin's are mighty slim.

OPPORTUNITIES, PLENTIFUL: There's just as good a fish in the creek as has ever been caught. • There's just as good a timber in the woods as has ever been cut.

OPPOSE: That goes against my raisin'.

OPTIMIST: Someone who starts putting on his shoes when the preacher says, "Now, in conclusion. . ."

OPTIMISTIC: As the Arkansas coon hunter said when asked how he was doin' after hunting all night: "This one I'm after now and five more'll make half a dozen."

OPTIMISTIC, OVERLY: He'd expect to bring home a bird from a wild goose chase.

ORGANIZE: Get your pigs in the pen.

ORGANIZED: I finally got everybody sittin' in the same pew.

OUT OF GAS, ALMOST: This pickup is runnin' on memories.

OUT OF PLACE: Lost. "She's as lost as a snowstorm in July."

OUT OF SHAPE: He looks like someone cut him open and stuffed him with Jell-O.

OUT OF TROUBLE, ALMOST: I finally got my ends meeting but I ain't quite got 'em tied yet.

OUT OF WORK: As a pregnant stripper.

OUT OF YOUR LEAGUE: You're a chihuahua tryin' to run with the big dogs.

OUTRAN ME: He went by me like I was up on blocks in the front yard.

OUTDOOR TOILET: Arkansas library. *See One-Holer*

OUTLOOK, DIFFERENT: The difference between a possum and a pig depends on who's doing the eating.

OUTMANNED: As one bug arguing with a flock of chickens.

OUTSTANDING: A real humdinger. "That new hydraulic jack I got for my wife is a real humdinger."

OVERACTIVE: Busy as a termite with a tapeworm.

OVERALLS: Arkansas tuxedo • Long-necked blue jeans • Bibbed (or bipt) overalls • Overhauls • Also called Big Bens. For the fashion conscious, overalls can be worn without a shirt in the hot summer months and with long-handle underwear and a sweatshirt or sweater in the cold winter months. In Arkansas, wearing underwear under your overalls is optional year-round but highly recommended.

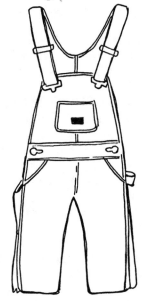

OVERATE: I'm stuffed plum to the gills.

OVEREXTEND: I got more baby pigs than my sow has spigots.

OVERKILL: Killed too dead to skin.

OVERLOOKED THE OBVIOUS: If it'd been a snake, it would a bit ya.

OVERREACTING: You're usin' a fryin' pan for a fly swatter.
• You're using dynamite for rat poison, which is usually pretty hard on the barn.

OVERSEXED: There ain't no neutral in her transmission.

OVERSTAYED THEIR WELCOME: The traditional Southern way of informing guests that they've stayed too long is to say, "I'm goin' to bed so you folks can go home."

P.B.R.: Pabst Blue Ribbon (beer), a favorite in the South.

Ph.D., ARKANSAS STYLE: Post Hole Digger

P.W.T.: Poor White Trash, what you strive not to be.

PACKED: Like pig's feet in a jar.

PAIN, SEVERE: That hurts worse than an anvil dropped on an ingrown toenail.

PALE: You look like ya been on a hayride with Dracula. •
Peak'd. "Bubba's lookin' peak'd since he got that IRS letter."

PANTING: Like a lizard on a hot rock.

PANTY HOSE: Arkansas tow strap.

PAPAWS: Arkansas bananas. Papaws are the yellow, edible fruit of the papaw (papaya) tree which is common in Arkansas.

PARENTAL AUTHORITY: A mama hen has the right to peck her chicks on the head if they need it.

PARENTS: In the South your parents are generally Mama and Daddy, no matter how old they are or how old you are. The collective form is "the folks."

PARENTS, BAD: Their son was born with a tattoo and it wasn't spelled correctly.

PARTICIPATE: If you ain't skinning, you can hold a leg.

PARTICIPATED: Had a hand in. "Joe Tom had a hand in turnin' over Judge Black's outhouse."

PARTY, DULL: It was about as exciting as a graveyard cleaning. A graveyard cleaning is an annual event where folks get together for a picnic and then spend the rest of the day cleaning up the graveyard.

PATCHWORK QUILT: Arkansas comforter. • Also called an "Arkansas Traveler," which is a patchwork quilt with individual units consisting of large squares made of four smaller squares, each of which is made up of seven small scraps. Each unit is a simple, straight edged shape designed to make maximum use of any available scrap.

PATIENT: As a settin' hen. She knows that what's comin' is inevitable and there isn't any way she can speed up the process, so she just squats patiently and waits.

PAY ATTENTION: Set your mind on it.

PAY FIRST: When I see the money in my hand, the goat'll jump off the wagon.

PECAN: A pah-con is a nut, a pee-can is what you use when you don't want to go to the outhouse in the middle of the night.

PENCIL WHIP: Pencil whipping occurs when the player keeping score fails to mark scores properly. In a friendly game, pencil whipping is humorous; in a money game it can be deadly.

PENMANSHIP: Hand. "Betty sure writes with a pretty hand."

PEROT, ROSS: Rawce PEA-row, the eccentric Texas billionaire who grew up five blocks from Arkansas. Mr. Perot came in third in the 1992 Presidential race, but history may one day suggest that Perot should be a national hero in the state of Arkansas, because without his taking votes away from George Bush, Bill Clinton might not have ever made it from an outhouse to the White House. While the people of Arkansas aren't ready to build any PEA-row statues just yet, if  they ever do, they'll probably make it life-size so they can save on bronze.

PERSEVERING: Hanging in like a hair in the biscuit.

PERSON: Body. "If our taxes are raised even a little bit, it'll be more than a body can stand."

PERSON, EDUCATED: He's book learned.

PERSON, GOOD: He's all wool and a yard wide.

PERSON, NOT NORMAL: He needs to go back into the oven and bake some more.

PERSON, OVERRATED: He was a self-made man before the days of quality control.

PERSON, SHIFTY: He's slicker than bus station chili. *See also Slick*

PERSON, SMALL: He could model for the figures on trophies.

PERSON, USELESS: His limitations are limitless.

PERSON, WORTHLESS: If you want to see how much he'd be missed if he died, just stick your finger in a pond, pull it out, and look in the hole.

PERSONAL RESPONSIBILITY: Every cat has to lick his own backside.

PERSUASIVE: He could talk a hen into pluckin' herself. A real persuasive person could talk that plucked chicken into jumping up and down on an ax to cut her own head off.

PHONY: As an Arkansas marriage license from Wal-Mart. • As an honest lawyer.

PICKUP: In the South it's just a pickup. It isn't necessary to include "truck" since everybody knows a pickup is something you drive, not something you find in a jukejoint. • Also called an Arkansas Cadillac.

PICKUP, NEW: It ain't got the novel wore off yet.

PICKUP AERODYNAMICS: True pickup aerodynamics is the measure of how well the pickup is designed to prevent tobacco pin-striping and juice blow-back when you spit out the window. A truck with good aerodynamics means you can spit out the window and the juice will land on the Mercedes that's tryin' to pass. Poor aerodynamics means when you spit at certain speeds it "blows back" into the cab or splatters along the side of the truck producing "tobacco pin-striping." Bad aerodynamics, especially when your wife is riding in the passenger seat, is when you spit out the driver's side window and the projectile travels around the cab and reenters through the passenger window. Such aerodynamics, if not corrected, are a leading cause of accidents and divorces.

PIGS, THIN: His pigs are so thin it'd take half a dozen of 'em to make a shadow.

PLACE TO SET: A hunker down spot.

PLAN: Aim to. "I aim to go to welder's school one of these days."

PLAN AHEAD: Build the coop before you buy the chicks.

PLANNING TO STAY: He's wearin' his sittin' britches.

PLAY DEAD: Play possum. "We thought Billy Fred was killed when that barn fell on him but he was just playin' possum."

PLEASED: Tickled to death. "I was tickled to death to only lose my garage when the cyclone went through my yard."

PLEASING: That's gooder 'n grunting.

PLEASURABLE: Ain't had this much fun since I fell in the waller with the hogs.

PLENTIFUL: As ticks in a wet spring.

PLIERS: Pinchers, so called because it's hard to use a pair of pliers for very long at one stretch without pinching a finger.

PLUCK A CHICKEN: Dress it. "Y'all come on over 'cause granny's gonna dress a chicken and fry it for supper."

PLUM: A popular Southern adjective that can be used to mean extremely, far, pleasurable, or almost anything else. "Bubba was plum crazy to go plum to Little Rock for a date with Mary Ann even though she is plum pretty."

PLUMBER, GOOD: He could plug Niagara Falls in half an hour.

POISE: The ability to look inconspicuous when you get to church late and have to walk down to the front row.

POKE SALAD: Poke salit, a leafy green vegetable that grows throughout the South.

POKER: Chips passing in the night.

POKER HAND, DANGEROUS: A Dixie Hammer, which is a poker hand of any five cards in one hand and a knife in the other. It's unbeatable unless the other fella has a gun, in which cause you become living proof that it ain't smart to carry a knife to a gunfight. Also called a Dixie Boxing Glove.

POKER HAND, WORTHLESS: An Arkansas straight. In poker, a normal straight is five cards in numerical order, such as 3, 4, 5, 6, 7. An Arkansas straight, which is good only for a bluff, skips one card between the others such as 3, 5, 7, 9, Jack.

POLITICIAN: Someone who has his snout in the public trough and who stands for what he hopes most people will fall for. • Politicians are like cockroaches. It's not what they carry off, but what they fall into and mess up.

POLITICIAN, AMBITIOUS: He's like a country dog in town, tryin' to pee on every post, which means he's trying to please everyone, which can't be done.

POLITICIAN, DANGEROUS: It's not what he don't know that counts but what he knows that ain't so.

POLITICIAN, DEVIOUS: He's so slick his socks won't stay up.

POLITICIAN, EXPERIENCED: He's like a football coach, smart enough to know the rules and dumb enough to think the game is important.

POLITICIAN, EXPERT: He can borrow $20 from you, keep it six months, pay you back only $10, and convince you it's even because you both lost $10. • If he was being chased down Main Street by a lynch mob, he could make you believe he was leading a parade.

POLITICIAN, GOOD: He can sit on a fence and keep both ears to the ground.

POLITICIAN, POOR: Once he makes up his mind he's full of indecision.

POLITICIAN, WINDY: He could give you mouth-to-mouth resuscitation over the phone.

POLITICS: The art of keeping as many balls in the air as possible while protecting your own. • You can break down politics into poly, which means many, and ticks which means bloodsuckers. Thus politics is many bloodsuckers.

POOR (FINANCIAL CONDITION): We're so poor we have to fast twice a week to keep from starving to death. • We're so poor we eat dried apples for breakfast, dried peaches for dinner, and then drink water for supper so the fruit will swell up and we can go to bed thinking we're full. • We eat so many collard greens we have to wrap coal oil rags around our ankles to keep off the cutworms.

POOR IMITATION FOR: Sorry excuse for. "Bubba, that poodle of yours is a sorry excuse for a bird dog."

POSITIVE: If it ain't true there ain't a possum or a poor person in Arkansas.

POSITIVELY: As sure as Santa Claus has reindeer manure on his boots.

POSSUM: A Southern game animal that ain't worth nuthin' till it's in a sack. There are a lot of possum recipes but here's the most popular: Clean and dress one middlin-sized possum. Put it in boiling water for half an hour to tenderize. Baste with honey and butter and stuff with medium-sized sweet  potatoes, carrots, and onions. Wrap in tinfoil and bake for one hour or until golden brown. Remove sweet potatoes, carrots, and onions and eat them. Give the possum to the dogs.

POT LIQUOR: Liquid that remains after cooking vegetables like greens. Nonalcoholic, chock full of vitamins, and good for sopping with a biscuit. Not to be confused with a pot licker, which is a faithful old hound dog that licks the pots clean after cooking so you don't have to wash 'em.

POWERFUL: A Southern adjective meaning very, immense, considerable, etc. "I'm powerful glad to get this check." • Also an adverb meaning deeply. "I'm prayin' powerful that the jury will come to its senses and not find mama guilty."

POWERFUL PERSON: If he crows it's daylight.

PREACHER, DEVOUT: He could pray a whole bowl of mashed potatoes cold just asking the blessing.

PREACHER, EMPHATIC: A suck-back preacher, which is one who frequently "sucks" large gulps of air for emphasis.

PREACHER, EXPERIENCED: He can predict the size of the collection just by looking over the crowd.

PRECARIOUS SITUATION: Your pig's sucking hind tit. Occasionally a sow will have more pigs than she has spigots. When that happens, one of the pigs usually has to settle for the hind teat, which means the other pigs are gonna get most if not all the milk before it gets to him, which is a precarious situation.

PRECAUTION: Never eat anything that grows wild around the back porch 'cause some folks don't always make it to the outhouse.

PRECIOUS: A term used by Southern belles to indicate a high compliment. "She just looks precious in that new dress." Synonyms would be darlin' and lovely. Antonyms would be sweet and nice, which Southern belles frequently use to sound nice when saying something is really tacky.

PREDICTABLE: No matter how warm the sunshine is, the cat will always have her kittens in the barn.

PREFAB: A house that is constructed elsewhere and assembled on your property. A prefab is sturdier and more expensive than a double wide, but you can't take a prefab with you when you move.

PREFERENCE: Druthers. "If I had my druthers, I'd drive a pickup instead of a mule."

PREGNANT: She looks like she swallowed a blimp seed.

PREGNANT AND SKINNY: She looks like a snake that swallowed a blimp.

PREJUDICED: Every ol' crow thinks her chicks are the blackest.

PREPARE FOOD: Fix. Folks up North may "prepare" dinner but Southerners fix it.

PREPARED FOR THE WORST: He never forgot how to pick cotton, which means if things get bad, he's prepared to pick cotton so he'll at least have a job.

PRESUMPTUOUS: Just because you donate an organ to the church, don't mean you call the tunes to be played.

PRETEND: Play like. "Why don't you play like you're a wrecker and haul your butt out a here."

PRICE: Worth. "What's that shotgun worth?" • What ya asking for it? "What ya asking for the bird dog pup."

PRIDE: Every old mother hen thinks her chicks are the best peckers.

PRIM AND PROPER: As a preacher's wife at a church social.

PRIORITIZE: Don't worry about rats in the barn when the hogs are in the corn.

PROBABLE: Likely as not. "Likely as not, Bubba'll be at the Dew Drop Inn tonight."

PROBLEM: We got fire ants in the outhouse.

PROBLEM, LARGE: There's a big crack in the dam.

PROFICIENT: Right handy with. "He's right handy with a fork."

PROGRESS, SLOW: All I'm doing is staying one day ahead of yesterday.

PROJECT IN PROGRESS: I got a hen on the nest.

PROMISCUOUS, HER: She's the busiest memory in town. • The inscription on her tombstone will read: "The only time she ever slept alone."

PROMISCUOUS, HIM: He won't ever buy a cow as long as he can milk one through the fence. • He ain't married but his wife sure is.

PRONE TO: Bad to do it. "Bubba's bad to fight after drinking some whiskey."

PROPOSAL, ATTRACTIVE: That'd get the preserves down on the bottom shelf.

PROSPEROUS: He's soppin' his biscuit in thick syrup.

PROTESTED: He raised a bigger stink than a skunk under the church.

PROUD: Glad. "I'm proud to meet you." • Laudable. "You shore did a proud thing when you made an honest woman out of Mary."

PUCKERED: Like a wet sheepskin next to a hot fire.

PUFFED UP: Like a frog in a cream can.

PULL DOWN YOUR DRESS: Stretch your gingham.

PULL UP YOUR PANTS: Hitch up your britches.

PUSH: Mash. In the South, you don't push a doorbell, you mash it. On the other hand, you don't mash a bug, you squash it.

PUTTING ON AIRS: Stepping high like a rooster in deep mud.

QUAIL: Quell, a popular game bird in the South. A bob-white quell is the most popular.

QUALIFIED: Earned his place at the fire.

QUALITY, FAIR: Middlin' fair. Although this saying is widely used to indicate average quality, that is not a correct usage. The term "middlin' fair" is actually a term in cotton grading used to mean the very best, a long way from average. The cotton grades, from very best to absolute worst, are: middlin' fair; good middlin'; strict middlin'; middlin'; and strict low middlin'.

QUALITY, GOOD: It's the best in all creation.

QUALITY, LACKING: That's all vine, no watermelons.

QUALITY, POOR: Piddlin' poor, which, in the South, is about as poor as you can get.

QUANTITY: A heap of • A sight of • Many a • A plenty • Right smart of • A whole passel of • A whole slew of.

QUICK LOOK: A windshield inspection, which means you just drive by it and look it over through the windshield of the car. Windshield inspections are frequently used when buying land.

QUICK TEMPERED: He can fly off the handle quicker than a minnow can swim a dipper. • His fuse is shorter than a chigger's eyebrow.

QUIET: You could hear the break of day. • You could hear a field mouse wetting on a cotton boll. • You could hear a worm's heartbeat. • You could hear your toenails growing.

QUIET TYPE: He don't use much kindling to get his fire started, which means he is a man of few words but the words he does use generally count for something.

QUIET WORKER: The hen that lays the biggest egg does the least cackling.

QUILT: Baptist pallet. *See also Patchwork Quilt.*

QUIT DRINKING: He weaned himself off the bottle.

QUITTING TIME: Time to put the tools in the truck.

R: A letter never used in the traditional old South unless it's at the beginning of a word.

R.C. COLA: *See Moon Pie*

RACCOON: Coon, a Southern game animal. Coon and collard greens is an Arkansas staple.

RACEHORSE, SLOW: You could time him with a calendar.

RADIATOR SHOP: The best place to take a leak.

RAG: Arkansas gas cap.

RAIN, HEAVY: A "clear up" rain, which means it rained so much the water was "clear up" to the door handles on a pickup.

RAIN, PROLONGED: A root soakin' rain, which means you got so much water the roots of trees were soaked thoroughly.

RAIN, INTERMITTENT: You could count the drops. • A three-inch rain, as in there was three inches between drops.

RAIN, SHORT: Lasted about as long as an old-timer's dance.

RAIN WHILE THE SUN IS SHINING: The devil is beating his wife.

RAIN GAUGE, COUNTRY STYLE: Chickens. If it starts to rain and the chickens run for cover, it won't rain long. If the chickens stay put, you are in for a long spell of rain because the chickens know they're gonna have to get wet sooner or later so they just keep pecking. Of course, before checking the chickens in Arkansas, they send the dog outside and if he comes back wet, they knows it's raining.

RARE MEAT: I've seen a cow cut worse than this get well.

RATTLES: Like marbles in a washtub.

RAZORBACK HOGS: Razorback hogs are generally as mean as a bear and more deadly because they travel in packs. It's been said that the most dangerous animal in the Arkansas hills is a razorback sow with a litter of pigs. These wild hogs, sometimes called "Long Rooters," have long snouts, long  tails, long tusks and a long squeal. The name comes from the fact the hog's back is long and thin, and appears to be sharp enough to shave with. Bill Clinton calls a razorback an "acorn chaser."

READY: She's combed her fur and tuned her purr. • He's primed and tightly wadded.

READY AS: A rooster with his spurs up.

REALLY?: "Sure 'nuff?" which is the reply when someone tells you something that's a little hard to believe. "You caught 45 fish, sure 'nuff?"

REAR END: Back of the lap • Hind end • Behind • Back porch

REAR END, LARGE: His butt's bigger than a river bottom coon. • If the button on her jeans ever pops off, her measurements will go from 38-24-36 to 38-24-and a whole bunch.

REAR END, SMALL: Scarce hipped. • He has to put a bed slat across the outhouse hole to keep from fallin' in.

REBEL YELL: A loud, often prolonged, yell that originated during the War between the States when Confederate troops were either charging or celebrating. The tradition of the Rebel yell is still alive in the South and can be heard often when Southerners are celebrating. To practice a Rebel yell, open a car door and then slam it on your fingers.

RECKLESS: As a mule kicking wasps.

RECKON: One of the most versatile words in the language of the South. It can be used for suppose, think, guess, believe, calculate, presume, expect, know, imagine, assume, speculate, etc.

RED: As a Carolina dirt road or a Rebel flag.

REDNECK: Once a derogatory term meaning "country bumpkin" or "poor white trash." Now "redneck" is commonly used to describe good ol' boys who love God, country, cold beer, hot romance, big guns, little government, slow dances, and fast horses, and they'll fight to defend any of 'em.

RELATED: They're blood kin, which means they are closer than kissing cousins.

RELATED, SORT OF: We're pea patch kin, which is a saying that originated from families, usually neighbors, that would pick peas together. • We're cow cousins, we were close enough to share a cow for milk but were not officially related.

RELATIVE, STRANGE: If you shook the family tree, he'd be the nut that fell out.

RELAX: It'll all come out in the wash.

RELIGIOUS FANATIC: He's got so much religion, he could hear the Pope's confession.

RELIGIOUS FREEDOM: The right to go to church or go fishing.

RELUCTANCE: I'd rather take out an alligator's appendix with a penknife than do that.

REMARKABLE: In the South, anything that is remarkable is "bodacious." "Bubba's the most bodacious welder ever."

REPAIR, TEMPORARY: Sharecropper repairs, which are repairs made with baling wire, black tape, duct tape, etc. Such repairs usually last just long enough to get you through the day.

REPAIRMAN, GOOD: He could repair the crack of dawn.

REPEATING: You've already whipped that old dog.

RESEMBLES, NOT MUCH: They look as much alike as Little Rock and Rome.

RESPONSIBILITY: It's your blister, you have to sit on it.

RESTRICTED: It's difficult to run with the big dogs when you're chained to the porch.

RESULTS, POOR: She did a lot a stirring but she didn't get many biscuits. • He did a lot of grinding but he didn't get much corn.

RETALIATE: Give back as good as you got or better.

RETIRE, EARLY: Go to bed with the chickens.

RIBS, BROKEN: His staves are sprung.

RICH: He's got more money than he can keep dry. • He's got enough to pay the Bill of Rights. • He could buy a boy for his dog.

RICH, BUT INEPT: "He was born with a silver foot in his mouth," which is how Texas Governor Ann Richards described George Bush.

RIDICULOUS: As asking a politician to guard your wallet.

RIDING FAST: He's riding fast enough to split a creek wide open.

RIGHTEOUS WOMAN: She always makes sure she gets caught doin' good.

RING: Rang. I heard the bell rang. • I gave her an engagement rang.

RISES FAST: As fertilized weeds.

RISES SLOW: As biscuits in a cold oven.

RISKY: You're dancing with the sheriff's girlfriend.

RIVER, DRY: The catfish raised a dust cloud swimming along the bottom.

RIVER, SHALLOW: A hog crossin' river, which means the hogs are walking across it. Although hogs can swim, they don't like to, so if the water is shallow enough, they walk.

ROAD, DIRT: Arkansas asphalt.

ROAD, ROUGH: A Tennessee freeway.

ROAD, WINDING: A moonshiner's road, which means there are so many twists and turns it's almost impossible for anyone to get close without being noticed.

ROCKING CHAIR: Gives you something to do but it don't get you nowhere.

ROLLING AROUND: Like a mule taking a dirt bath.

ROOM, COLD: You could use it as a deer locker.

ROOM, CROWDED: There ain't enough room left for a shadow.

ROOM, LARGE: You could drill a regiment in it.

ROOM, SMALL: There ain't even any room for sunshine to come in the window.

ROPE, LONG: Enough to hang all the wash in Tennessee on.

ROYAL CROWN COLA: *See R.C. Cola*

RUIN, IMMINENT: The weevils are in the cornmeal.

RUNNING AROUND: Like a chicken with its head cut off.

RUNS AROUND: Like a pumpkin vine.

RUNS FAST: As panty hose in a briar patch.

RURAL: We lived so far out in the country the sun knocked a brick out of the chimney every time it went down. We live so far out into the country we don't get Monday Night Football till Wednesday morning.

RURAL ROAD, ARKANSAS STYLE: Rural roads in Arkansas are where "traffic is noted for not bein' present." Also applies to many roads in Tennessee.

S.E.C. The Southeastern Conference, of which both the University of Arkansas and the University of Tennessee are members.

SAD: Would jerk tears from a glass eye. Would make an Italian statue cry.

SAD PERSON: He's so down in the mouth he could eat oats out of a churn.

SAFE: As a coon in a hollow log.

SALAD, PLAIN: Garden sass, which is basically a plate of fresh vegetables served straight from the garden. May include greens, onions, tomatoes, cucumbers, etc. but no dressing of any kind; just wash 'em, cut 'em up, and put 'em on a plate.

SALESMAN, GOOD: He could sell autographed pictures of George Bush in Hope, Arkansas.

SALESMAN, POOR: He couldn't sell watermelons at a roadside stand even if the Arkansas State Police was stoppin' traffic for him. • He couldn't sell hacksaw blades at the state prison.

SALT PORK: Arkansas chicken, which means folks in Arkansas eat it about as often as the rest of the world eats chicken.

SASSAFRAS TEA: A potent tea made from the bark of the sassafras tree. It's so potent it's sometimes called "blood thinner." In Arkansas, it's used to eliminate the weak.

SATISFIED: As a full hound dog sleepin' in the sunshine.

SATURDAY: Butter 'n egg day, which is the day country folks go to town to sell butter and eggs for money to be spent on essentials.

SAW: Seen. "I seen who shot the jukebox."

SAY GRACE: Ask the blessing.

SCARCE: As a white shadow. • As pig tracks on a white linen tablecloth.

SCARECROW, ARKANSAS STYLE: A rubber snake. This comes from the belief that crows are afraid of snakes, so if you put a couple of rubber snakes in your garden, they'll stay away. The theory assumes crows are stupid enough not to notice the "snakes" never seem to move around.

SCARECROW, EFFECTIVE: That's such a good scarecrow the crows are bringing back the corn they stole last year.

SCARECROW, WORTHLESS: The crows are nesting in its armpits.

SCARED: The butterflies in my stomach have butterflies.

SCARED DOG: That dog was so scared he ran with his tail curled up so tight his hind legs were lifted off the ground.

SCARED OF THE DARK: Take the broom with you, which is a standard reply of Southern mothers when their children are afraid to go to bed or the outhouse because of darkness. The implication is they can use the broom to ward off the boogie man.

SCARY: That made my butt pucker so hard I had to use a crowbar to get my jeans out of the crack.

SCRATCHED UP: He looks like he crawled through a barbed wire fence naked to fight a bobcat in a briar patch. • He looks like he stumbled and fell into a blender.

SCRATCHY: As burlap sheets. • As tow sack bloomers. • As a stucco bathtub.

SCREWDRIVER: Arkansas ice pick.

SECOND TABLE: Where the children eat when company comes calling.

SECURITY SYSTEM, ARKANSAS STYLE: A mean dog and a loaded shotgun.

NOTIS
THIS PLACE PURTECTED
BY A BITIN DOG AND A
SHOTGUN THAT AIN'T
LOADED WITH FEATHERS

SECURITY SYSTEM YARD SIGN, ARKANSAS STYLE

SEDUCTIVE LOOK: It'll melt the fillings in your teeth.

SEEMS: 'Pears to me; "It 'pears to me that the buck you shot looks a lot like a milk cow."

SELF-CENTERED: She's a real foot stomper. Southern ladies are very prone to stomping a foot whenever they don't get what they want or when things don't go to suit them. It is widely believed that Southern women are taught to stomp a foot immediately after they take their first step. Hillary Clinton was not born in the South, but she has ways of getting her way.

SELF-EMPLOYED: He's dangling on his own hook.

SELF-TAUGHT: Jackleg, such as jackleg plumber.

SELF-WORTH: She thinks she's the only show pig in the pen.

SENSE OF FAMILY: He knows where his grandparents are buried.

SENTIMENTAL: She'd even kiss a ghost good-bye.

SET YOUR GOALS HIGH: Eagles don't chase mosquitoes.

SETTLEMENT: We split the biscuit and both got a half.

SHAKING: Like a dog passin' a peach pit.

SHALLOW RIVER: I've seen dew deeper than that.

SHARE CROPPING: Farming on the halves (or thirds or fourths, depending on the deal).

SHARE RESPONSIBILITY: You do the shellin' and I'll do the shuckin'.

SHIRT SLEEVE: Arkansas handkerchief.

SHIVAREE: An Arkansas (or Southern) wedding celebration.

SHIVER: Whenever you shiver it's considered a sign that a possum just ran over your grave.

SHOOK UP: As milk in a runnin' cow.

SHOP RAGS: Red rags, even if they're blue or white or purple.

SHORT LIVED: As a jug at a barn raisin'.

SHORT PERSON: You could smell earthworms on his breath.

SHORT TIME: About as long as you can hold a bear's tail.

SHOW DOWN: When push comes to shove.

SHRUNK: Drawed up. "When she washed my new shirt it drawed up something fierce."

SHUCK MATTRESS: A mattress made from corn shucks instead of feathers.

SHUCK MOP: A mop made by twisting dampened corn shucks into holes in a piece of wood.

SHUT UP: Why don't you put some teeth in that hole.

SICK: I'd have to get better to die.

SIGHT, IMPAIRED: He couldn't see through a pig fence. • If he ever needs stronger glasses, he'll have to switch to a seeing eye dog.

SILLY: As a goose. A goose is so silly that when it rains he'll stand still with his head up and drown if not saved.

SIMPLE ISSUE: According to Bill Clinton, a simple issue is one where "you don't have to be smart as a tree full of owls to understand it." Examples of simple issues would be the national debt and foreign policy.

SIMPLE MINDED: He's like a goose, he wakes up in a different world every day.

SINGER, POOR: He can carry a tune just fine, but he gets into real trouble when he unloads it.

SINNER, REFORMED: From now on, the only thing he'll be guilty of is singing too loud in church.

SIPHON HOSE: Arkansas credit card.

SITUATION, PERPLEXING: It's too slow for possum and not fast enough for coon.

SITUATION, POOR: He's like an Arkansas mule, no ancestry and no hope for posterity.

SITUATION, SERIOUS: The wringer's broke and it's wash day at the orphanage.

SIZZLED: Like a lizard struck by lightning.

SKEPTIC: If it looks like manure and smells like manure, a skeptic would have to taste it to be sure it is manure.

SKEPTICAL: As a fat hog on a frosty mornin'. *See Weather, Cold*

SKINNY ANIMAL: Looks like a gutted snowbird.

SKINNY MAN: You could use him for a dipstick. • He can shower in a rifle barrel. • He's nuthin' but breath and britches.

SKINNY WOMAN: She could walk through a harp and not strike a note. • She has to wear suspenders to hold up her girdle. • She ain't nuthin' but breath and bloomers.

SLANTING: Cattywhampus • Antigoglin • Slaunchways • Slantindicular • Skewgee • Kittycornered.

SLAP HARD: Put his head in a sling. "Mary Lou slapped Bubba so hard, she put his head in a sling."

SLICK: As a wet watermelon seed.

SLICK PERSON: In the South, someone who is slick is a person capable of talking out of both sides of his mouth at the same time, which means what you think you hear him saying is not necessarily what he means. Politicians are frequently referred to as slick.

SLIDE: The past tense, according to Dizzy Dean, is slud. "He slud into second base headfirst."

SLOW: As steam rising off a fresh cow patty on a cold morning.

SLOW MOVER: You'd have to catch him by a post to see if he was moving. • She'd have to speed up to stop.

SLOW WITTED: He's convinced "duh" is the third letter of the alphabet.

SMALL AMOUNT: Smidgen • Dust of • Piddlin' amount.

SMALL BABY: Arm or lap baby, which is one so small it's either in a crib, in your arms, or on your lap.

SMALL FEMALE: If she was gold plated you could use her for a watch fob.

SMALL HEAD: He could look through a keyhole with both eyes at the same time.

SMALL PERSON: He was picked before he was ripe.

SMALL THING: That's about as big as the little end of nothing whittled to a point.

SMART: He may have been born at night but it wasn't last night.

SMELL, STRONG: It's stronger than perfume at a high school dance.

SMILING: Like a dead hog in the sunshine. When a hog is slaughtered and laid out in the warm sunshine, his skin will draw up giving the impression he is smiling.

SNORING LOUD: Sounds like a rip saw running through pine knots. • Snoring loud enough to knock plaster off a wall. • In parts of the South, when someone is snoring he's said to be "Callin' his hogs."

SNOW, DEEP: The snow was so deep we had to sit down on a shotgun and shoot ourselves up the chimney to get outside.

SNUFF: Worm dirt, so called because it looks like the dirt worms are packed in at bait houses. The preferred unit of measure is "pinch." *See also Chewing Tobacco*

SOO-EE: A pig call farmers use when calling their pigs. The call would actually go something soo-ee, soo-ee pig, sooooo-ee, sooooo-ee soo-ee pig. • The call used by Arkansas fans to inspire their football team, the Razorbacks. • The new White House call to a staff meeting.

SOP: The preferred Southern way to eat gravy or syrup. Simply take a biscuit, dip it (or sop it) in gravy or syrup, and eat.

SOP GRAVY: A gravy made by mixing water (no flour) with the juices and some of the fat of fried meat.

SOPHISTICATED: A sophisticated Southerner is one who can quote Shakespeare without crediting it to the Bible. In Arkansas, a sophisticated person "has been places and 'et in hotels."

SORE: I feel like a cow that was milked by Captain Hook.

SORGHUM: A light colored molasses made from juice pressed out of sorghum cane and cooked. The residue after cooking is "blackstrap," a dark molasses with a sharp, tart taste. Distilled sorghum cane syrup is called "monkey rum."

SOUR: That's so sour it'd pucker your innards.

SPEAKER, EXPERIENCED: He can give directions without using his hands.

SPEAKER, LONG WINDED: He goes around the steer twice to get to the horns (or points).

SPEECH, TOO LONG: A really long speech is a stem winder, which means it lasts so long you'll have to wind your watch before it's over.

SPEECHLESS: As a youngster run over by a calf.

SPEEDING: He's goin' faster than a bat out of Georgia.

SPELLER, POOR: He has to look on his driver's license to spell his own name.

SPEND TIME WISELY: Do a lot more peckin' than cacklin'.

SPINNING: Like a dog with a clothespin on his tail.

SPLATTERED: Like a cow peein' on a flat rock.

SPREAD OUT: Like a sneeze through a crocheted handkerchief.

SPRING: Arkansas (or Tennessee) water fountain 'cause all you have to do is lay down and dunk your head. A sophisticated Arkansas water fountain is one where someone has driven a stake into the spring and attached a tin can or dipper that can be used to drink from.

SPRING, YEAR ROUND: A spring that flows year round is an "everlasting spring."

SQUARE MEAL, ARKANSAS STYLE: Whatever you killed in the morning, served on toast.

SQUEAKS: Like the springs in a fat woman's bed.

SQUEALED: Like a baby pig caught under a gate.

STANDS OUT: Like an ostrich in a hen house.

START OVER: Go back to the chicken pen and learn how to scratch.

STARVING: I'm so hollow inside, if I fell down, I'd explode like a dropped light bulb.

STATISTICS, FALSE: Those figures have been cooked a little too long.

STAY CALM: Hold it in the road, which is what we all hope Bill Clinton will do.

STAY CLOSE: Stick to him like pine tar to an Arkansas road.

STAYED IN BED: Stood. "My dinner wasn't ready 'cause my wife stood in bed all morning watching soap operas on TV."

STAYS CLOSE TO HOME: I've been back under the house looking for eggs farther than she's been away from home.

STEAK, TENDER: This steak is so tender I don't see how it held the cow together.

STEER: The difference between a bull and a steer is that a bull has his work cut out for him and a steer has had his works cut out.

STEP LIVELY: Like a rooster in a bed of hot coals.

STICK OF WOOD: Arkansas pencil. A stick of wood makes a great pencil when you need to do some drawin' or cipherin' and all you got to write on is dirt.

STICKS: Like stink to manure • Like a tattoo.

STICKY: As Arkansas pine tar.

STIFF: As a frozen hoe handle.

STINGS: Like whiskey on a cut finger. In the hills, moonshine is frequently used as an antiseptic for small wounds, and the sting is so bad it's worth not gettin' cut just to avoid the treatment.

STINGY: She was so stingy she wouldn't put an egg in her cornbread.

STOCKS, WORTHLESS: Ain't good for nothing but wallpaper in the outhouse.

STOB: An Arkansas radiator cap. A stob is a small piece of wood, whittled to a sharp point so it resembles a short, wide stake. Stobs can be used to fix almost anything that has a hole in it or to replace any kind of stopper.

STOMACH, LARGE: He looks like he's got a second grader under his shirt.

STOMACH, FULL: You could crack a tick on his stomach, which is usually said of children after having a meal at grandma's house.

STOOD OUT: Like a tall man at a Japanese funeral.

STOP AT: Go by. "Joe Tom, can we go by the drugstore?" In the South it is important to remember that when you go by a place you don't actually pass it, you stop there.

STOP SIGN: Arkansas target.

STRANGE PERSON: He ain't workin' with a full string of lights. • He ain't wrapped too tight.

STRANGER: I wouldn't know him if he walked in and played *Nearer My God To Thee* in whole notes on a mouth organ.

STRONG ARMED: He could throw a pork chop past a hungry coyote.

109

STRONG PERSON: He could tear up an anvil with a feather and have the feather left. • He could tie a bow knot in a crowbar.

STRUTTING: Like a tomcat walkin' in sorghum.

STUBBORN: As a rusty pump, which is mighty stubborn about giving water. • As a $2 Arkansas mule.

STUBBORN FEMALE: She's got a body like a marble statue and a head to match.

STUBBORN MALE: He'd argue with a pork barrel.

STUCK: Like a cow in quicksand.

STUCK UP: Her nose is so far up in the air a dirt dauber is liable to build a nest in it.

STUDENT, POOR: They had to burn down the schoolhouse to get him out.

STUFFED: As a ballot box in a Democratic primary.

STUPID MAN: He saw some baby pigs sucking on mama and thought they were blowing her up. • He opened a tall man's shop in Tokyo. • He'd hold a fish underwater to try to drown it. • He would take a duck to a cockfight and bet on him. • He'd hitchhike on an airport runway.

STUPID WOMAN: She used his food stamps to mail a letter. • She don't know if she's washin' or hangin' out. • Food for thought gives her indigestion.

STUPID FEMALE: She has to sneeze every now and then to keep the dust from building up inside her head.

SUCCESS: Is being able to tell the truth at your high school reunion.

SUCTION, GOOD: Could pull a peach through a garden hose.

SUCTION, POOR: Wouldn't pull a loose feather off a chicken.

SUGAR TIT: A small amount of sugar tied up in the end of a cloth. Makes a great pacifier for babies.

SUMMER: What follows spring; never a verb in the South.

SUPPOSE: Reckon. "Do you reckon the Hogs will ever win the SEC championship?" • Spect. "I spect the Hogs will win the SEC someday, but I ain't sure it'll be in my lifetime."

SURPRISED: As a pup with his first porcupine. • As a car chasin' dog that caught a Buick.

SURPRISED RESPONSE: Well, look a here. • Y'shut yo' mouth. *See also Embarrassed Reply*

SURPRISING: That'll make the back of your dress roll up like a runaway window shade.

SUSPICIONS: The stove is cold but the woodpile is shrinking, implying someone is stealing wood.

SUSPICIOUS AS: A goat eyeing a new gate.

SWAMP SUCKER: A low-life person from Georgia but the expression can be used to describe any low-down person.

SWEATING: Like a scalded hog.

SWEEP: Arkansas it, which means run a broom over it and move the dirt around a little bit.

SWELLING, REDUCED: Swayge down. "I hope my sprained ankle will swayge down so I can play in the game this week."

SWOOPED DOWN: Like a hen hawk on a nesting quail.

TTACKY: A favorite Southern word that has multiple uses. Tacky is used to describe outlandish attire. "Mary sure looked tacky in those green knock-me-over shoes and purple pedal pushers." • Tacky is used to describe rowdy behavior. "I've never seen Fred when he wasn't acting tacky." • Tacky is also used when someone is causing embarrassment to another person. "Bubba was so tacky to Mary she cried herself to sleep."

TAKE A CHANCE: You can't fry an egg without breaking some shells.

TAKE ACTION: Rock or get out of the chair.

TAKE IT TO THE LIMIT: See how close you can get to the fire before ya get burnt.

TAKEN: Took. "Mary Lee had her picture took."

TALENTED PERSON: He could lay a straight fence with crooked rails. Frequently, in the hills, fence rails were crooked, so anyone who could lay a straight fence with them was talented.

TALK: Visit. "The sheriff wants to visit with you awhile."

TALK NICE: You get more hogs in the pen by throwing corn instead of rocks.

TALKATIVE: She puts out so much hog chatter that she has to oil her jaws to keep 'em from seizing up.

TALKING BIG: You're spreading more manure than all the cats in Arkansas could cover up.

TALKS LOUD: He learned how to whisper in a sawmill.

TALKS TOO FAST: She talks so fast you could use her tongue for an egg beater.

TALKS WITHOUT THINKING: Shoots from the lip.

TALL PERSON: If he fell down, he'd be halfway home.

TANGLED UP: Like a barrel full of fish hooks.

TASK, LARGE: I was one hand short of having enough to do that, which means it was a job for two people instead of one.

TASTE, EXPENSIVE: He's got California taste and an Arkansas pocketbook.

TASTES BAD: That tastes like it was dipped out of a sour hog trough.

TASTES GOOD: That'd make you slap your granny for more.

TEACH: Learn. "He had to learn his dog not to be afraid of possums."

TEACHER, POOR: He couldn't teach a chicken to peck.

TEETH, LARGE: He could bite through a side of bacon and not grease a lip.

TEETH, STRONG: Arkansas bottle opener.

TELEPHONE CABLE SPOOL: Arkansas coffee table.

TELEPHONE STATIC: There's a dead cat hangin' on the line somewhere.

TELL IT ALL: Wring all the water out of the rag.

TELL ME MORE: Put some more kindlin' on that fire.

TELL THE TRUTH: Don't let the grease burn in the skillet, which implies if you lie, the skillet will heat up and burn the grease.

TELLING THE TRUTH: You ain't just whistlin' *Dixie*.

TEMPER TANTRUM: *See Conniption Fit*

TENNESSEAN: Sometimes called a Mudhead.

TENSE: He's wound up tight as a pea vine through a picket fence. • Her nerves are tighter'n a cotton clothesline after a soaking rain.

THANK YOU: In the South, you'll usually hear much obliged, 'preciate it, or bless your heart, a favorite among grandmothers.

THAT EXPLAINS IT: That accounts for the milk in the coconut. This expression is used when something you don't understand is explained to you. It comes from the fact that one of the mysteries of Arkansas (and other places) is how in the world did that milk get inside that coconut.

THIEF: He sells hogs that ain't exactly his to sell. • He'll steal anything that ain't too heavy or too hot to carry.

THIEF, QUICK: He could steal the moon hubcaps off a moving pickup.

THIEF, STUPID: He'd try to hold you up with a caulk gun.

THICK HEADED: If he got shot between the eyes, it'd take the bullet half an hour to make a hole.

THICK SKINNED: The doctor would have to use a hacksaw to take out his appendix.

THIN PERSON: His skin flaps on his bones like a quilt on a clothesline.

THINGS DON'T CHANGE: Whether you wink at 'em or kiss 'em, don't make the pigs any cleaner.

THIRSTY: I'm so dry, I'd have to be primed to spit.

THIS: This here. "This here is the pickup we used on our honeymoon deer hunt."

THREATEN A CHILD: Southern mothers traditionally threaten their children with, "If you can't listen, you can feel" which means if the child doesn't listen to what he's supposed to do, he can feel the switch when it's applied to the back of his lap. If mother ain't home, daddy will use "I'm gonna wear you out if you don't do what I tell you."

THREATEN HER: I'm gonna knock you so cold that by the time you wake up your clothes will be out of style. • I'll hit you so hard your kids will be born shaking.

THREATEN HIM: I'm gonna hit you so hard that it'll raise a knot on your head so big you'll have to stand on a step ladder to scratch it. • I'm gonna hit you so hard you'll wear out bouncing. • I'm fixin' to open up a can of surefire whupass.

THROW: Chunk. "Trust her as far as you can chunk her."

THUMP-SSSS: The sound you hear when a water moccasin drops out a tree limb into the bottom of your boat. Generally followed by one or more splashes as the fishermen bail out.

THUNDER: God's tater wagon tumped over.

TIGHT FIT: Tight as last year's longhandles.

TIGHTWAD: Swimming was invented when he came to a toll bridge.

TIME, INDEFINITE: A spell. "It's been quite a spell since the Tennessee Volunteers won a national championship."

TIRED: Plum tuckered • Wore slap out • Played out • Tired to death • I ain't got much giddy up in my get along.

TIRED AS: A sharecropper's mule on a hot day.

TIRES, WORN: They're so thin you can see the air inside.

TO EACH HIS OWN: Some people object to a fan dancer, others object to the fan. • A cow chip is a buffet to a fly.

TODDLER: Yard baby, which is one you can let wander around the yard while you're hoeing the garden.

TOILET SEAT, USED: Arkansas picture frame.

TOLERANCE: Ability to listen to another person's fish or hunting story and not try to top it.

TONGUE-TIED: His tongue got caught on his eyeteeth and he couldn't see what he was saying.

TOO CLOSE TO THE PROBLEM: When you're sittin' in it you don't smell it.

TORNADO: Cyclone to old-timers and mountain folks.

TOUGH: As a sow's snout • As white leather, which is the tough leather used to make harnesses for draft horses.

TOUGH JOB: It'll take a lot of river water to float that boat. • Like trying to drive a swarm of bees through a snowstorm with a hickory switch.

TOUGH PERSON: He's even got a tattoo on the roof of his mouth.

TOWN, BORING: The most exciting thing to do is sit around and watch a pickup rust.

TOWN, SMALL: They don't even have a cannon in the park, which, for a Southern town, means it is really small. • So small they had to widen the street to paint a stripe down the middle of it. • A hick town, which is one that ain't even close to being on the bus line.

TOWN, STRICT: Girls can't buy a bra without a prescription.

TRAFFIC SIGNAL: Traffic signals in the South are red lights even though they also have green and yellow lights.

TRAIPSE: In the South, traipse is used to mean "wander about." "We had to traipse all over town lookin' for a pair of shoes that'd fit Bubba."

TRAPPED: Like a lizard under a cow patty.

TRUTHFUL: If I ain't telling the truth I hope to kiss a cow and smile.

TRAVELER, POOR: His idea of a long trip is havin' to walk halfway 'round the campfire to get to the handle on the coffee pot.

TRIED BUT FAILED: He did a lot of shootin' but he didn't get any meat.

TROUBLE: A worrysome situation. *See In Trouble*

TROUBLE, SERIOUS: You got an ox in the ditch.

TROUBLE, UNEXPECTED: I got trapped on a high bridge by an unscheduled train.

TROUBLE BREWING: The storm clouds are gathering.

TRUSTWORTHY: If he says a hen dips snuff, you can look under her wing for the can.

TRY, HALF-HEARTED: He gave it a lick and a promise.

TRY IT: Sling it against the wall and see if it sticks.

TRYING THE IMPOSSIBLE: You're trying to shovel sunshine.

TURN OVER: Tump over. "I'm gonna shoot that dog next time he gets after a rabbit and tumps over my still."

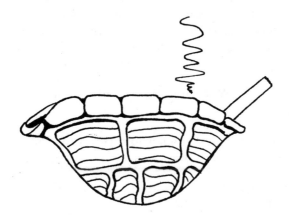

TURTLE SHELL: Arkansas ashtray.

UGLY: As mud fence. In Arkansas (and other places) fences were occasionally made using "bricks" of mud mixed with straw and then dried. Really ugly fences!

UGLY BABY: He's so ugly, his mother had to put an Elvis mask on him before she could nurse him.

UGLY CHILD: If she ever gets kidnapped, they won't put her face on milk cartons 'cause it would ruin the milk business. • He's ugly as Ned in the first grade reader. An old-time school book used to teach reading had a character named Ned who was truly ugly.

UGLY ENOUGH: To clabber a mud hole.

UGLY MAN: He's so ugly all the flies stay on his side of the pickup. • He has to slip up on a mirror to shave. • When he was young his daddy had to tie a pork chop around his neck to get the dogs to play with him. • His funeral procession will have to go down the alley. • He couldn't get a date in a women's prison.

UGLY WOMAN: You wouldn't take her to a dog fight even if she was favored to win. • When her husband goes out drinkin' he takes her picture so he'll know to stop drinking when she gets good looking. • The only time she looks good is when you're lookin' at her through the bottom of an empty beer glass.

ULYSSES S. GRANT: "Useless" S. Grant to most Southerners.

UNATTAINABLE: That's one possum you won't get into a sack. • That's one fish you'll never see on a stringer.

UNCHANGEABLE: You can take the boy out of Dixie but you can't take Dixie out of the boy.

UNCOORDINATED: He can't rock and chew at the same time. • If he fell out of a boat, he couldn't hit the water.

UNCOUTH: He'd build an outhouse in the front yard. • She'd wear knee-high stockings with a short dress.

UNDERESTIMATED: You're callin' an alligator a lizard.

UNETHICAL: He'd shoot quail on the ground.

UNEXPECTED: As a fifth ace.

UNFRIENDLY: As a mule on a sawdust diet.

UNINFORMED: What I know about that could be engraved on a boiled peanut.

UNIVERSE: Tarnation. "He's the best shot in all tarnation."

UNLIKELY: Far fetched. "It'd be pretty far fetched to think somebody from Hope, Arkansas could get elected President."

UNLUCKY: If he bought a cemetery, people would stop dying.

UNRELIABLE: Only count on him when the goin' is easy.

UNSOPHISTICATED: He came in on a load of watermelons.

UNSURE: I ain't sure I understand all I know about that.

UNWANTED: I need that like a chicken needs spit.

UP TO DATE: There ain't no flies on him.

UPBRINGING: Your "raisin'" in the South.

UPPITY: She thinks she's the show pig in the pen.

UPSET: I was so mad I wanted to kick the dog and spit.

UPSTAGED: Somebody stole the clap out of my thunder.

URINATE: Drain your crankcase. • Milk a snake. • Shake the dew off the lily.

USE SPARINGLY: Don't use all the kindling on one fire.

USELESS: As a steering wheel on a freight train • I got no more use for that than Noah had for a fog horn on the ark. • As an ashtray on a motorcycle.

V

V.I.P.: A tree shaker • A big bug.

VACILLATE: Crawfish, which, in this case, is used to describe someone who has made a firm decision, then changed his mind.

VAIN: I wish I could buy her for what she's worth and sell her for she thinks she's worth.

VALUE, LITTLE: That's like owning a sawmill that don't make 2 X 4s. Any sawmill that didn't make 2 X 4s, the most popular size of cut lumber, would not be worth much.

VALUE, SMALL: It's worth about as much as an Arkansas diamond. Arkansas is one of the only places in America where you can dig for diamonds. Unfortunately, even if you find one, it won't be worth near as much as a regular diamond.

VERY: Powerful; "I'm powerful glad to have a job." • Mighty; "I'm mighty happy with the election results" • Plumb; "I'm plumb proud of Billy Fred." • Durn; "I'm durn happy to see you." • Downright; "He's downright smart."

VETERINARIAN, GOOD: He could cure a bear skin rug.

VICE PRESIDENT: Texan John Nance Garner said it best with, "The Vice Presidency isn't worth a bucket of warm spit." *See also Gore, Al*

VICINITY: In these parts • Hereabouts • In this neck a the woods.

VICTORY: We rolled over 'em like a cow rocking on a flat pea.

VIEW, PLEASANT: That's a sight for sore eyes.

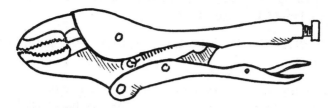

VISE GRIPS: Without doubt, a pair of Vise Grip pliers is the most versatile tool a country boy can own. Vise Grips can be used to hold a muffler on your pickup; as a wire stretcher; as a clamp; as an emergency diaper pin; fish hook remover, and 100s of other uses. One Arkansas man even used Vise Grips when he lost the steering wheel off his pickup and they were still working fine three years later when he sold the truck.

VISITOR, INFREQUENT: He comes around about as often as Elvis does so we call him Eclipse.

VOICE, DEEP: His voice is so low you can smell socks on his breath.

VOICE, GRAVELLY: Sounds like he gargled with axle grease.

VOICE, HIGH: Sings like she has one foot caught in a steel trap.

VULNERABLE: As a duck froze to a pond.

 WALK CAREFULLY: Like a chicken with an egg broken inside.

WALK PROUDLY: Sashay. "I'm gonna sashay down to the barber shop and show off my new boots."

WALK SEDUCTIVELY: She's got more moves than a snake caught in a bear trap. • She's got more moves than Allied Van Lines.

WALKING ROCKER: A walking rocking chair is one that moves just a smidgen (little bit) each time you rock back and forth. If you're not careful, it'll walk right off the porch.

WANT TO KNOW: I'd give my upper plate to know that. Upper plate refers to false teeth.

WANT TO STAY YOUNG: I don't want to be a blessing. *See Old Person*

WARM: Burnin' up, which means you're too hot to be comfortable. "I wish I hadn't wore three pair of longhandles 'cause I'm burnin' up."

WARM AS: A grandmother's blanket.

WASHTUB: Arkansas bathtub

WASP: Mud dauber • Dirt dauber • Hornet • Yellow jacket.

WASTED EFFORT: You can train a jackass all you want, but you ain't ever gonna see him in the winner's circle at Hot Springs.

WASTEFUL: As a busload of lawyers going over a cliff with three empty seats.

WASTING BREATH: You're talking to Noah about high water.

WASTING MONEY: Burning rocket fuel in a coal oil lamp.

WASTING TIME: You're shuckin' a nubbin. A nubbin is a tiny, useless ear of corn that grows near the top of the stalk and which would be a waste of time to shuck.

WATCH OVER: Mind. "Will you mind the kids awhile."

WATCH WHAT YOU SAY: Chickens tend to come home to roost, which is country for "words can come back to haunt you."

WATER, DEEP: The water got so high grandpa was shooting ducks in the parlor and grandma was catching catfish in the kitchen mousetrap.

WATER, MUDDY: Too thick to drink, too thin to plow. • The fish had to swim backwards to keep from gettin' mud in their eyes.

WATER, POOR: You have to chew it before you can swallow it.

WATER MOCCASIN: Usually just "moccasin" 'cause Southerners know where they come from.

WATERY: Loose. "Her stew is always real loose."

WAYNE, JOHN: The Duke, a true Southern hero.

WE: In Arkansas and Tennessee, especially in the rural areas, you'll frequently hear "we'uns" for we.

WEAK PERSON: He couldn't lick his upper lip.

WEATHER, CLEARING: It's fairin' up.

WEATHER, COLD: It's hog killin' time. Before the days of deep freezes, cold weather was the preservative. Hogs were butchered when the first cold snap signaled winter was on the way.

WEATHER, HOT AND DRY: Sick dog weather, which is a reference to a sick dog's nose being dry and hot instead of cold and wet as usual.

WEATHER APPROACHING: It's comin' up a cloud. • The sky is clabberin' up.

WEATHER CHANGE, SUDDEN: Came on so sudden that when the boiling water froze the ice was still warm.

WEATHERMAN, POOR: The only things he can predict correctly are sunup and sundown.

WELCOME: A Southern welcome is "Make yourself at home."

WELL ACQUAINTED: I know him better'n I know my old broom.

WELL, DEEP: That well's so deep it must a been dug by a banker who dropped a nickel down a gopher hole.

WENT BAD: Went back on his raisin', which is often said of a preacher's child who turns out bad.

WENT BROKE: Lost everything but the dirt under my fingernails.

WENT TO WORK: Hard on. "I hard on down at the chicken processing plant 'cause I heard you could buy chickens for half price once they'd been dropped on the floor."

WET: It was so wet we had to put hip boots on the hogs.

WHAT'S HAPPENING? What in the Sam Hill's going on?

WHAT'S WRONG? What ya got stuck in your craw?

WHATEVER: Everwhat. "Everwhat you want to do is fine with me and any ol' gal I'd go out with."

WHATEVER SUITS YOU: Whatever tweaks your beak.

WHEELBARROW: Arkansas buggy.

WHEN: Southerners rarely just say "when." Usually it's when ever. "When ever are you'uns comin' over to the house?"

WHEN ALL IS SAID AND DONE: Lou Holtz, former coach of the Arkansas Razorbacks, said it best: "When all is said and done, as a rule, more is said than done."

WHICHEVER: Everwhich. "Everwhich way you like it."

WHISKEY: There are three kinds of whiskey: hugging, singing, and fighting.

WHISKEY, STRONG: That'd make a bullfrog spit in the eye of a moccasin. • It'll jump your IQ fifty points per swallow. • Makes anyone who drinks it a hero.

WHISTLING WOMAN: According to an old Southern saying, "A whistling woman and a crowin' hen will come to a bad end."

WHO: Who all. "Who all's goin' to the poker game?"

WHO'S IN CHARGE: Who's skinning this possum?

WHO MADE YOU MAD? Who licked the red off your candy?

WHO WON: Who beat. "I didn't see the fight, who beat?"

WIFE: A wise man once observed that wives are like state fairs, they get bigger and better every year.

WIFE, GOOD: I wouldn't trade her for twelve acres of pregnant red hogs.

WIFE, IDEAL: If you fell asleep watching football on TV, she'd remove your chaw of tobacco so you wouldn't choke to death.

WIGGLE: Like a lizard in a skillet. • Like a worm on a hook.

WILD AS: A peach orchard boar.

WILL FIT PARTS: "Will fit parts" are those that are not original replacement parts but which "will fit," so to a Southern country boy they will work.

WILLINGNESS: If you want butter, you gotta be willing to churn.

WIND, STRONG: The tomatoes wouldn't grow because the wind kept blowing the sunshine off the vines. • Blowin' so hard a chicken laid the same egg three times.

WINDBAG: He could blow up a blimp.

WINDOW, OPEN: Pneumonia hole on a car; juice hole on a pickup.

WINDSHIELD: WINN-shield, sometimes called windersheild in Tennessee.

WISE MAN, ARKANSAS STYLE: A wise man in Arkansas is one who never locates the source of his whiskey, especially if it's moonshine. Even though moonshining isn't as prevalent as it once was, it's still "wise" not to wonder off into some strange parts of the Arkansas hills.

WITH CERTAINTY: Without fail. "You gonna pay me back that ten dollars without fail, right?"

WOBBLED: Like a model A Ford with a flat tire • Like a red wagon with three wheels • Like a drunk on a bicycle.

WOMAN, MAD: Hell on high heels.

WOMAN, NOT SO TOUGH: I've seen wilder heifers than her milked into a gourd.

WOMEN: Are like cow patties, the older they are, the easier they are to pick up.

WON, BARELY: We out sorried 'em, which means neither team played well but somebody had to win.

WOOD, QUICK BURNING: Breakfast wood. Some wood, like dry pine, burns very quickly, allowing only enough time to cook breakfast and not enough time to cook a large meal like supper.

WOOD, SLOW BURNING: Supper wood. Some wood, such as oak and hickory, burns slow and thus provides enough fire to cook a large meal.

WORDS OF COMFORT: I'm sure you'll feel better once it quits hurting, which is a standard among Southern mothers.

WORKED TOO LONG ON A PROJECT: You've been dragging that same cotton sack too long.

WORKER, GOOD: He keeps his corner up, which means he does his share of the work.

WORKER, HARD: He don't even stop working to catch his breath, which is considered a true Southern compliment.

WORKER, POOR: When he walks up it's about the same as three good men leaving.

WORKING END: The business end or the blister end.

WORKING HARD: As a cat trying to shake off a pinching worm.

WORRIED: He's wearin' out the floor, which means he's doing a lot of pacing.

WORRIED A LOT: I'm sleeping like a baby; I wake every two hours and cry.

WORRY HIM: Drop him in the grease, which means give him something to worry about.

WORSHIPER, ARDENT: He has a reserved seat in the amen corner.

WORTHLESS: Nothing you'd want to work up a sweat getting.

WORTHLESS AS: A pile of possum tails • Cold snail tracks.

WORTHLESS PERSON: He ain't worth the oxygen he uses up.

WOUNDED SEVERELY: Lost enough blood to paint the porch.

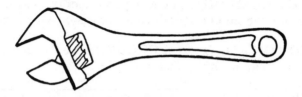

WRENCH, CRESCENT TYPE: Arkansas socket set.

WRINKLED: As a cheap suit in a cheaper suitcase. • He's got more wrinkles than a washboard.

WRONG: That ol' dog won't hunt.

X-RAY: Ax-ray picture or bone picture. One of the great mysteries of the South is how does that Ax-ray camera see through hide.

YAM: Although the terms "yam" and "sweet potato" are used interchangeably, a yam is not a sweet potato. When sweet potatoes are candied in the South, they become yams.

YANK: Southerners don't "yank" anything, they "jerk" it.

YANKEE: A euphemism for damn Yankee. A lot of Southerners are in their teens before they know damn Yankee is two words. Southerners generally use "Yankee" to mean anyone who isn't a Southerner.

YANKEE DIME: Many use Yankee dime to indicate a quick kiss. For others, the term is derogatory to Yankees. As the story goes, following the War for Southern Independence, Yankee troops would demand credit from the few remaining Southern stores and then hardly every pay back as much as a "Yankee dime." Many Southerners still use phrases like "He ain't worth a Yankee dime" to describe someone who doesn't pay his obligations.

YANKEE VISITOR (IN WINTER): Snow birds.

YARD EGGS: Eggs found in the yard rather than in a nest, which are usually considered inferior to nest eggs.

YELLOW: As a summer squash. • Pale green to Southern ladies who speed through a traffic light on yellow.

YES: Southerners rarely just say yes when asked a question and the answer is obviously yes. They use phrases like: Does a one-legged duck swim in a circle? Does a chicken have a pecker on his head? Is a frog's butt waterproof?

YES, DEFINATELY: Yes siree, Bob. • You sure as hell got that right. • I'm here to tell ya. • You betcha.

YOU: It's almost always pronounced "ya" in the South.

YOU ALL: One of the great arguments in the South is whether or not "y'all" can ever be singular. Some say yes, others no. To be sure you're using it in the plural, say "all y'all." • In the hills, and sometimes in the cities of Arkansas and Tennessee you'll also here "you'uns" for you all. Just like y'all, you'uns can be used for singular or plural.

YOU ARE WELCOME: Southerners frequently don't bother to include the "are" and just say "you welcome."

YOU CAN DO IT: Even the smallest dog can bury a big bone.

YOU UNDERSTAND? You hear? "Don't call me again, y'hear?"

YOU'RE ABSOLUTELY CORRECT: Ain't that the truth.

YOU'RE LATE (FOR A MEAL): "You missed the blessing," which is what many Southern mothers say when you're late for a meal. The meaning is clear; mama ain't happy and like they say in the South, "When mama ain't happy, ain't nobody happy."

YOU'RE RIGHT: You hit that nail right on the head.

YOU'RE WRONG: If that's what you think, you got another think coming. • You're pullin' the wrong dog's ears.

YOUNGSTER: His teeth ain't wore down much.

YOUR CHOICE: Grab a skinnin' knife, grab a leg, or grab your butt and haul yourself out'a here.

YOUR RESPONSIBILITY: If your dog trees it, you gotta skin it.

Z **ZERO:** Ought • Nuthin'. An Arkansas radio announcer once reported the results of a scoreless football game by saying, "We won, ought to nuthin'."

ZIPPER: Barn door.

ZIPPER, OPEN: Your barn door is open. • The lid on your snake cage is open. • Your cotton is blooming.

THE END: Preachin's over.

SECTION TWO

Say it Like a Southerner

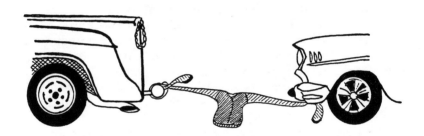

PANTY HOSE: Arkansas tow strap

Rules for Speaking Proper Southern

1. Never pronounce the "g" in words ending in ing. "My arthritis is so bad I can't do any more huntin', fishin', or woman chasin'."
2. To add rhythm to your speech, put an "a" in front of those words you cut the "g" off of. "How could I fish when it was a-thunderin' and a-lightnin' and a-hailin' so bad."
3. No matter what you're talking about, folks, firearms, fish, farm animals, anything really, put an ol' in front of it.
4. For most words, the emphasis will be on the first syllable such as INsurance, ASHtray, CAWfee.
5. Occasionally, you'll have to add a letter, such as "a" in athlete for athalete or subtract a letter such as the "r" in throw for thow.
6. The letter "t" should be used creatively. Occasionally it will replace the "ed" as in ruint for ruined or skint for skinned. A "t" is also frequently added to words that end in "s" such as acrost for across or unlest for unless.
7. If you're in the deep, traditional South and want to sound like you were raised on a plantation, never pronounce the letter "r" unless it is at the beginning of a word.
8. When asked a question you don't immediately know the answer for, begin your reply with "well" stretched out to about four syllables so you have a few seconds to think of an answer.
9. To avoid making a commitment, use words like should and ought to instead of can or will. "The engine in that ol' pickup ought to last for a few more thousand miles and the tires should be good enough to carry you for those miles."
10. When talking to a Southerner, don't get too close and never put your hand on him to make a point. Never stare him in the eyes for a prolonged period of time, unless you want him to assume you're lying. Glance around the room often while continuing to talk.
11. When speaking, talk slowly and with some deliberation.
12. Although you should talk slow, that shouldn't keep you from running some words and phrases together, as in "zat rite" for is that right, "jew" for did you, and "I'd a" for I would have.
13. And finally, to offset running some words together, pronounce other words as if they had several extra syllables such as um-bur-el-ah and are-thur-eye-tis.

A LOT: fourdy-leven dozen
ABOUT: 'bout; near 'bout
ABOUT TIME: high time
ACCURATE: ack-rut
ACE OF SPADES: asa spades
ACHE: a painin'
ACT: play possum
ADDRESS: AD-ress
ADMIRE: mighty fond of
AFFLICTED: eat up with
AFTER WHILE: directly;
   toreckly
AGAINST: agin'
AGE SPOTS: old lady freckles
AGGRAVATION: agger-vation
AGRICULTURE: agger-culture
ALABAMA: Al-ah-baam-ah
ALL: allest
ALL MY LIFE: all my born
   days
ALLOW: 'low
ALLOWANCE: 'lowance
ALMOST: aw-most; like to
ALUMINUM FOIL: tin-foal
AMBULANCE: am-blance
AMERICAN: Umurkin
AMONG: amongst
ANNOYING: warting
ANOTHER: unuth'r; whole
   nuther
ANT HILL: ant bed
ANTIFREEZE: annafreeze
ANTS: aints
ANXIOUS: chompin' at the bit
ANYTIME: any day and time
APPEARS: 'pears
APPLY: dab it on
APPRECIATE: 'preciate
APT: liable to
AREN'T YOU: arn-cha
ARGUE: argy
ARITHMETIC: cipherin'
ARKANSAS: Ar-KIN-saw

ARKANSAS PEOPLE: Arkies;
   ArKANsans; Arkansasan,
   Arkansawer
ARMADILLO: armadilla
ARMFUL: armload
ARROW: err'a
ASKED: ast
ASPIRIN: ass-burn
AT ALL: atall
ATHLETE: ath-a-leet
ATLANTA: Et-lanna
ATTACK: light into
AUNT: ain't
AUTHORITY: a-thar-ty
AUTO: awe-toe
AUTUMN: awe-dumb
AWFUL: awflest
BACK: bayuk
BACK OUT: azzle out
BACKWARDS: bassackwards
BACKWOODS: upbrush
   country
BAD: bayud
BAG: sack
BALD: ball-headed
BALLOON: bloon
BARBECUE: barb'q; bobby'cue
BARBECUE STAND: pig stand
BARBED WIRE: bob wahr
BAREFOOT: barefooted
BARREL: bar'l
BASS BOAT: loveboat
BASS FIDDLE: bull fiddle
BATTERY: batry
BE COURAGEOUS: keep your
   dauber up
BEANS: banes
BEAR: bar
BECAME ILL: took sick
BECAUSE: 'cause or ba-cause
BED: bay-ed
BED BUG: chinch bug
BEEN: bin

133

BEFORE: 'fore
BEGINNING: the get go
BEHAVE: BE-hay've; mind ya' manners
BEHIND: bah-hind
BELONG: blong
BESIDES: sides
BEST: bestest or bay-ust
BETWEEN: 'tween
BIBLE: marryin' book
BILOXIE: Blux-ee
BIRMINGHAM: Burminham
BLACKEYED PEAS: cow peas
BLEW: blowed
BLUEJAY: jaybird
BOIL: a risin
BOILING: ballin
BORROW: bar'ry
BORROWED: bard
BOTH OF THEM: boffum
BOTHERSOME: worrisome
BOWLEGGED: shanksprung
BRA: flopper stopper
BRA, LARGE: bowling ball bag
BRAG ABOUT: brag on
BREAD: light bread
BRIAR: brar
BROKEN: busted
BROUGHT: brung
BULB: bub
BURLAP BAG: tow sack; feed sack; gunny sack; croker sack
CAFE: CA-fay
CALL ME: give me a holler
CAN NOT: kaint
CAN'T YOU: cane chew
CAREER: crear
CASH: cash money
CAT: cayut
CATCH: ketch
CAULIFLOWER: colly-flar
CAVALRY: calvary
CENTER: sinner

CEREAL: seer'l
CERTAIN TO: bound to
CERTAINTY: cert-ney
CHAIR, CANE BOTTOM STRAIGHT BACK: settin' chayer
CHAIR: chayer
CHANCE: chaince
CHANGE (coins): egg money
CHARLESTON: Chal-stun
CHEST OF DRAWERS: chester drawers
CHEVROLET: Chivverlay
CHEVY SUBURBAN: redneck limousine
CHICKEN: yard bird
CHICKEN HAWK: hen hawk
CHILD: tricycle motor
CHILD'S TOY: play pretty
CHIMNEY: chimley
CHINQUAPIN: chinkypin
CHOIR: kwarr
CHORUS: coarse
CHRISTMAS: Chrismus
CHURCH: meetin' house
CHURCH SERVICE: prar meetin
CICADA: jarfly
CIGAR: sea-gar
CLAIMED: allowed as how
CLAWS: dinner hooks
CLEAN: clane
CLEAN SHAVEN: bald faced
CLEAR: as mother's milk
CLERK: counter hopper
CLIMBED: clum
CLUMSY: tangle-footed
COCA COLA: cocola; cocoler
COFFEE: caw-fee; belly wash
COIL: coa-all
COLD: col
COLLECT: klect
COLUMBIA: Ka-lumb-ya

COME HERE: comere
COME ON BACK: moan bac
COMMON SENSE: horse sense
COMPANY: kump-knee
CONFESSED: fessed up
CONFUSED: twitty-patted
CONTAGIOUS: catchin
CONVENIENCE STORE: ice haouse
CONVENIENT: handy
CORN: cawn
CORNER: CAWN-er
CORRECT : creckt
CORSAGE: CAR-sodge
COTTAGE CHEESE: clabber cheese
COUCH: sofa
COUGH: the croup
COUNTRY SONG, SAD: a bleeder
COWARD: ka'rd
COYOTE: ki-yote
CRAZY: bat brained
CREEK: crick
CRITICIZE: critter-size
CROOKED: whopperjawed
CRYING: crine
CURRENT: curnt
DANCE: daintz
DANCING: hog rasslin'
DARK OUTSIDE: pitch black
DARLING: darlin'
DEAD: day-ud; daid
DEAF: as a cow skull
DECEMBER: Dee-ceym-bur
DEFENSE: DEE-fense
DENTURES: store bought teeth
DEPUTY: dep'tea
DIAGONALLY: catty corner
DIAPER: three corner pants; hippins
DICTIONARY: word book

DID YOU: jew
DID YOU EVER: jevver
DID YOU HAVE TO: chafta
DIDN'T INTEND TO: did'n go to
DIP BREAD IN GRAVY: sop
DIRECTLY: d'rectly
DISH CLOTH: dish rag
DISH TOWEL: cup towel
DISORGANIZED: frazzled
DISTRAUGHT: tore up
DITCH: gulley ditch
DO IT CHEAP: poor boy it
DO YOU WANT ANY? y'ontny
DOG: dawg
DON'T YOU: don'cha
DONKEY, MALE: a jack
DOUBLE BARREL: dub'l barl
DOWN: daoun
DOWN TO: downt
DREAMED: drempt
DRESS SHOES: Sunday shoes or hard shoes
DRESSED UP: gussied up
DRINK: drank
DRIZZLING: mizzling
DUSK: first dark
DUST: house moss
EAR DRUM: hear drum
EDUCATION: edge-cation
EIGHT: ayut
EIGHTEEN: a't-tane
EIGHTY: aid-ee
ELECTION: leck-shun
ELECTRICITY: lec-tricity
ELEVATOR: flyin room
ELEVEN: levin
ELSE: ailse
EMBROIDERY: em-brawd-ry
EMPLOYEE: hand
ENCOURAGE: brag on him
ENGLISH: Ainglish
ENTIRE: inn-tar

135

ERRAND: aaron
ERUPTED: broke out
EUROPE: Yur'p
EVAPORATED MILK: canned cream
EVENING: eve-nin
EVENTS: goings on
EVERLASTING: as Dixie
EVERY: ever
EVERYTHING: ever'thang
EXCEPT FOR: seppin
EXCEPT: sep
EXPECT: 'spect
EXTRA: extry
EXTRAORDINARY: doozey
EYE: ah
FAMILY: fam'ly
FAN: fayan
FAR: fur
FARM LABORER: hand; hoe hand; field hand
FARMER, SMALL TIME: a wool-hat boy
FARMER: Agro American
FAST: lickety split
FAT: hen plump
FATIGUED: plum tared
FAVORS: resembles
FEBRUARY: Feb-er-wary
FEED MILL: grist mill
FENCE: feeunce
FIFTEEN: fahf-tane
FIFTH: fee'th
FIFTY CENTS: four bits
FIGURE: figger
FILM: feel'm
FINGER: fanger
FINGERNAILS: claws; love hooks
FIRE: far
IREARMS: far'arms
FIREFLY: lightnin' bug
FIREPLACE: far-place

FIT FOR: fitten
FLATTER: sugar mouth 'em
FLORIDA: Flar-duh
FLOWERS: fl'ars
FOLLOW: faller; bird dog 'em
FOOL: fu'al; yokum; yahoo
FOR: f'r
FOREIGNER: furiner
FOREST: woods
FOREWORD: foard
FORGET: fer-git
FORTY: foe-ar-dee
FOUR: foe-are
FOURTEEN: foe-are-tane
FREEZING: frazin
FRENCH FRIES: Franch fries
FRESH: frash
FRIDAY: Fry dee
FRIENDLY: neighborly
FRIVOLOUS: fritter-minded
FROM HERE: fum'mere
FRONT YARD: frunt-chard
FROSTING: icin'
FROWNING: knittin' his eyebrows
FROZEN: froze
FRYING PAN: skillet
FUNERAL: berry'in
GARLIC, WILD: ramp
GATE: gay't; gap
GENERAL: GIN-rul
GENERALLY: giner'ly
GENUINE: gen-u-wine
GEOGRAPHY: jogger-fee
GEORGIA: Jaw-ja
GET CLOSE: sidle up
GET READY: prime the pump; rosin the bow
GET: git; fetch
GIN: gee-un
GIRDLE: pot holder
GIVE UP: say uncle

GIZZARD STRING: stomach
tendon
GLANCE AT: cut your eyes to
GO FOR IT: go fart
GO HOME: go to the house
GO SLOW: drag your anchor
GO TO: run to
GOING TO: gonna
GOLF: cow pasture pool
GOOD-BYE: bye, bye
GOT AWAY WITH: got by with
GOVERNMENT: guver-mint
GOVERNOR: guv-ner
GRANTED: granite
GRAVEYARD: marble orchard
GREEN: grain
GREEN BEANS: snap banes
GREET, INFORMALLY: pass
howdies
GRITS: gree-uts
GROWING: feathering out
GUARANTEE: gar-un-tee
GUITAR: get-tar; getfiddle
GUITAR PLAYER: picker
GUTS: insides
HAD TO: had'da
HAM: hay um
HAND ME: reach me
HANDBAG: pocketbook
HANDLE: blister end
HANDS, SOFT: city hands
HANG CLOTHES: string 'em
HARD JOB: rough row to hoe
HARMONICA: mouth organ
HASN'T IT: had-n-it
HAY: horse manure seeds
HEAD: noggin
HEADACHE MEDICINE:
easin powder
HEARD: hear'd
HEARD ABOUT: hear'd tell of
HELL: hay-ul
HELLO: hay; howdy

HELP: hep
HEMORRHOID:
hammer-royed
HERO: HE-row
HICKORY NUT: hickernut
HIGH HEEL SHOES: knock-
me-over shoes
HIGH: as a peckerwood hole
HIGHWAY HEAT WAVES:
witch-water
HILL: he-yull
HIMSELF: is-say-eff
HIRED: Hard
HIT ON HEAD: conk him
HIT: A lick
HOE: cotton chopper
HOE COTTON: chop
HOG FOOD: slop
HOLD: holt
HOLDING HANDS: armed up
HOLLOW: holler
HOMEMADE: ho'made
HONEYDEW MELON: mush
melon
HONKY TONK: hawn'ky
tawnk
HOPEFULLY: hope-flea
HORNET: harn-it
HOTEL: HOE'tell
HOUR: ar
HOUSE: haouse
HOW: haow
HOW ARE YOU: har-ya
HOWEVER: howsomever
HUMAN: humun bee-in
HUNDRED: hunnert
HYDRANT: faucet
HYMN: he-um
HYSTERICAL: slap happy
I AM: I'se
I DECLARE: I swan
I DIDN'T: ah'din
I DON'T KNOW: I-ont-no

I SUPPOSE: I reckon; I'magin
I WOULD HAVE: I'd a
ICE: ahce
ICED TEA: ahs tea
IDEA: eye-dear or idy
IDENTICAL: spittin' image of
IDIOT: idjit
IF: iffen
IF I WAS YOU: fize-you
IF YOU: few
IF YOU WANT TO: if y'wanna
IGNORANT: IG-nert
ILLEGAL: EEL-eagle
ILLEGITIMATE CHILD: a
  briar patch kid
IMPORTANT: IM-pore-dunt
IN ALL DIRECTIONS: every
  which a way
IN DISREPAIR: misfixed
INAPPROPRIATE: ain't fittin'
INCH: ainch; ainches
INDEBTED TO: beholden to
INJURED: stove up
INSTANTLY: sudden like
INSTEAD OF: sted-a
INSURANCE: IN-surance
INTEND: aim to
INTERESTED: innersted
INTERESTING: innerrestin
INTERSTATE: innerstate
INTESTINES: innurds
INTRODUCE: inner-duce
INVITATION: in-vite
IRISH POTATOES: arsh-taters
IRON: arn
IS THAT RIGHT: zatrite
ISN'T: Idd'n
IT'S ALL RIGHT: sawright
IT: hit
ITALIAN: EYE-tal-yun
JAGGED: jaggedy
JAIL: jay-ul
JAPAN: Jay-pan

JAPANESE: Jap-knees
JIMMY: GMC pickup
JOKED: scalped his goat
JOKING: funnin
JULY: Jew-lie
JUST: gist
KEROSENE: coal oil
KILL: keel
KILLED: kilt dead
KIND OF: kind a like
KINDLING: lighter wood
KISS, QUICK: a Yankee dime
KNEES: prayer bones
KNIFE: naff; pig sticker
LADIES PARTY: hen party
LADLE: dipper
LARD: pig salve
LAST NIGHT: las nite
LATER: treckly
LAXATIVE: working medicine
LEADER: big frog in the pond
LEARNED OF: got wind of
LEAVE: light out
LEFT: lay-uft
LEG: laig
LEGS, LONG: he's high
  rumped
LET GO: turn a loose
LET'S: less
LET'S SEE: lessee
LIABLE: lie-bull
LIAR: lahr
LIBRARY: lie-berry
LICENSE PLATES: tags
LIGHT: laht
LIKE: lahk
LIPSTICK: pucker paint
LITTLE ROCK: Liddle Rock
LOG, HOLLOW: gum
LONELY: lonely hearted
LONG JOHNS: lawnghandles
LOOK ALIKE: spittin' image
LOOK THERE: lookie yonder

LORD: Lard
LOUISIANA: Luzy-ann-ah
LOUISIANA NATIVE: coonass
LUNCH: dinner
LYING: line
MAD: riled up; fit to be tied
MAD AS: a wet hen
MAD ENOUGH TO: eat bees
MADAM: ma'am
MAKE FUN OF: throw off on
MAKE ROOM: scotch over
MAKESHIFT: jakeleg
MAKEUP: war paint
MAN: mayon
MANY: minnie
MARINES: M'reans
MARRY: jump the broom
MATERIAL: ma-tear-ul
MATERNITY BLOUSE: slip
    cover
MAYONNAISE: man-aze
MEMORIZE: mem-rize
MEN: menfolk
MENOPAUSE: minner-paws
MERINGUE: calf slobber
MESS WITH: tinker with
MESS: a real mare's nest
MESSED UP: boogered up
METHODIST: Meth-dis
MIDWIFE: granny woman
MIGHT: maht; libel to; mite
    could
MILD: maul'd
MILE: mall
MILK: sweet milk
MILK A COW: pump a cow
MILLION: me-yun
MINNOW: minna; minner
MIRACLE: meer-kul
MIRROR: mere
MISERY: mix-ree
MISSISSIPPI: Mis-sippy

MISSISSIPPI RIVER: the big
    muddy
MISSOURI: Ma-zur-ah
MOCKINGBIRD: mocker
MOLARS: bridle teeth
MONDAY: Mun-dee
MONTGOMERY: Munt-gum'ry
MOON, FULL: buttermilk
    moon
MORE THAN: more'n
MOSQUITO: skeeter
MOST: lion's share
MOTHER: Mama
MOUNTAINS: maountins
MOUTH: bug hole; tater trap
MOVING FAST: ginnin; a
    flittin
MOW THE LAWN: cut it
MRS: miz
MUD DAUBERS: dirt daubers
MUD, STICKY: post oak mud
MULE, STUBBORN: jar head
MUSHROOM: toadstool
MYSELF: ma-self
NAKED: nekkid
NASHVILLE: Nigh-ish-vul
NATURALLY: natch-urly
NECK PAIN: crick in the neck
NEED: hurtin' for
NEGOTIATING: dickering
NEVER MIND: nemmind
NEW: brand spankin'
NEW ORLEANS: Nu'ar' leans
NEWNESS: novel
NEWSPAPER ARTICLE: a
    piece in the paper
NEXT: nex
NICKEL: case nickel, instead
    of five pennies
NINE: nahne
NINETEEN: nahne-tane
NIT PICKING: picayunish
NO: naw; nope

NONE: not a blessed one
NONSENSE: hog wash
NOON, EXACTLY: high noon
NORTH CAROLINA: Nawth
  Cara-linah
NOT ABLE: can't hardly
NOT ANY: nary a one
NOTHING: nuthin'
NOW 'N THEN: ever wunst in
  a while
NOW: naow
NUCLEAR: nooclar
NURSE: pan handler
OBEDIENT: minds
OBSOLETE: ob-sleet
OBSTACLE: stump in the row
OF: a
OFF OF: offen
OFFICER: awf-sir
OIL: awl; Texas tea
OKRA: okrie
OLD-FASHIONED: old-timey
OLD: ol'
ON FIRE: a far
ON HIS SIDE: sidin' with
ON TOP: atop
ONCE: wunst
ONLY: onliest
OPERA: opry
OPOSSUM: possum
OPPOSITE: op-set
ORANGE: arnge
ORDER: awder
ORNERY: on-ree
OTHER: tuther
OTHER SIDE: yonder side
OUGHT TO: auta; orta
OURS: ars
OUT OF PLUM: geehawed
OUTHOUSE: backhouse
OVER THERE: oh-vare; over
  yonder

OVERALLS: oh-vrals;
  overhauls
OVERFLOWING: sloppin' over
OWL: al or hoot al
PAINS: miseries
PALE: peaked
PANTS, SHORT: high water
  britches
PANTS, SNUG: tight butt
  pants
PARADE: prayed
PARLOR: front room
PARTICULAR: pa-tick-erly
PARTNER: pardner
PASS GAS: break wind
PASS: payus
PASSION FLOWER: ground
  ivy
PAY NO ATTENTION: pay no
  never mind
PEAS, WITHOUT PORK:
  motherless peas
PECAN CANDY: pray-lean
PEN: ink pen
PERCH (FISH): panfish
PERSIMMON: Ozark date
PESTER: pick at; worry him
PHYSICAL: fizz-cul
PIANO: pee-anna
PICTURE: pitcher
PIECE: a chunk
PILLOW: pill-ah; piller
PINE RESIN: rozzum
PINK: pank
PINTO BEANS: red beans
PLEASE: play-ze
PLIERS: plars; pinchers
PNEUMONIA: lung fever
POCKET KNIFE: apple peeler
POETRY: poe-tree
POISON: pizzen
POKE: jab
POLICE: PO'leece; p'leese

POLITICS: poly-ticks
PONDER: study
POODLE: poodle dog
POOR: pore
PORK (FATTY): fatback
PORK SKINS: cracklin's
POTATO: tater
POWER: par; pyre
POWER-LINE POLE:
   high-line pole
PRANCED: sashayed
PREACHER: Bible thumper or
   pulpit pounder
PRECISE: perzackly
PREFER: ruther
PRESERVE FOOD: put up
PRETTY: purr-dy
PRIVY: outhouse
PROBABLE: prob-ly
PROCRASTINATE: piddle
   diddle
PROPER: fitten
PROTRUDING: pooched-out
PROVOKE: aggervate
PUMPKIN: pun-kin
PURE: hard down
PURSE: pocketbook
PUSSY WILLOW: possum
   bush
PUZZLED: buffaloed
QUARREL: quarl; cuss fight
QUARTER: two bits
R.C. COLA: R.O.C. CoCola
RACCOON: coon
RAIN, LIGHT: a spittin' rain
RAIN, SOFT: angel tears
RANCH: rainch
RASCAL: yahoo
RASH: prickly heat
RATHER: druther
REALIZE: rill-eyes
REALLY: rilly

REAPPEARED: bobbed up
   again
RECALL: I'm minded of
RECKON: suppose
RECOGNIZE: reck'anize
RED: ray-ud; rad
REFRIGERATOR: ice box
REGULAR: reg'lur
RELATIVES, DISTANT: last
   cousins
RELATIVES: kin; the folks
RESEMBLES: favors
RESIN: raw-zin
RESTAURANT: res-trunt
RESTART IT: recrank it
RESTING: layin' up
RETIRE: re-tar
REVENUERS: reven-oors
REVERSED: bassackwards;
   the hind parts front
RHEUMATISM: roomytism
RHUBARB: pie plant
RIBS: staves; smack bones
RICE: swamp seed
RIGHT HERE: ratcheer
RIGHT THERE: ryte thar
RING: rang
RINSE: wrench
ROAD, SMALL: pig trail
ROCKING CHAIR: rocker
RODEO: row-dee-o
ROUGH LOOKING: grizzled
RUINED: ruint
SACK: poke
SAFETY PIN: latch pin
SALE: sayul
SALT PORK: fatback; sowbelly
SANDWICH: sam'ich
SANTA CLAUS: Sanna Claws
SATURDAY: Sadderdee
SCARED: skeert
SCARS: hero tracks
SCATTER: spew

141

SCIENTIST: sign-tist
SCORPION stinging lizard
SCREEN: scrane
SECOND: secont
SEE YA later: I'll be talkin at ya
SEEMS 'pears
SEEN ENOUGH: got an eyeful
SELL: sayul
SEMI: SEM-eye
SERVING: helping
SEVEN: sebum
SEVENTEEN: sebum-tain
SHADE: a black spot
SHADOW: shad-a; shadder
SHAKY: rickety
SHALLOW: shaller
SHARECROPPER: wool-hat boy
SHAVEN: slick faced
SHINY: as a new pie pan
SHOOT: far
SHOP AT: trade with
SHOULD: oughta
SHOULD NOT: best not; ought not
SHOW OFF: strut your okra
SHOWER: shar
SICK: ailish
SIDEWAYS: slaunchways
SILO: grainery
SINGLE: sangle
SIREN: sigh-reen
SISSY: panty waist
SIT DOWN: siddown
SIX: saxs
SIXTEEN: saxs-tane
SKELETON: one rack
SKIN: hide
SKINNED: skint
SKULL: head bone; conk
SKUNK: polecat
SLOP PAIL: thunder-bucket

SMALL AMOUNT: smidgen
SMALLEST: least'un
SMELL: smayul
SMILE; small
SNEAKED: snuk
SNUFF: worm dirt
SOBER: as a corpse
SOFT DRINK: sody; sody water
SOLDIER: sojer
SOME ARE: summer
SOME MORE: smore
SOME OTHER: smother
SOMETHING: sump'n
SOON: directly
SOONER OR LATER: by and by
SOOTHED: salved over
SORE: a gall
SORT OF: sort'a; kinda like
SOUTH: saouth
SPARE TIRE: spar tar
SPARSE: slim pickens
SPENT: petered out
SPIKE: spack
SPILLED: spil't
SPIRITED: feisty
SPIRITUAL: spear-chule
SPITTOON: spit can
SPRING: sprang
SPRINGTIME: struttin' and gobblin' time
SQUARE DANCERS: dosey doers
SQUASHED: smushed
SQUAT: hunker down
SQUEAMISH: lily livered
SQUIRREL: mountain boom'r
STALLED: hemmed 'n hawed
STALLING: spittin' on the handle
STARE: fix eyeballs
START: crank it
STAYING: stain

STAYS: pickets
STEEL: stayle
STEEL BAR: jobber
STIFF: stove up
STILL: a rig
STILTS: tom walkers
STORM CELLAR: fraid hole
STOVE: lizard scorcher
STRAW: broomweed
STREAM, SMALL: creek
STRING, SHORT: piggin' strang
STRING: strang
STRIPPED: stripe-ed
STRONG: stout
STUFFING: dressin'
SUITABLE: fittin'
SUNDAY: Sun dee
SUNRISE: sun up
SUNSET: sun down
SUPPOSE: spose
SUPPOSED TO: sposta
SURE THING: lead pipe guaranteed cinch
SURE: shore
SUSPECT: spect
SUSPICIOUS: spish-us
SWALLOW: swaller
SWAMP: sunk land
SWEARING: cussin'
SWEET POTATO: sweet tater
SWEET POTATO PIE: new-ground pie
SWITCH OFF: cut off
SWOLLEN: pooched out
SWUNG: swang
SYRUP: sur-up
TABASCO SAUCE: Cajun catsup
TAKE A BREAK: shade up
TAKE SNUFF: dip
TAKEN: took
TALK BAD: poor mouth

TALK, FOOLISH: shine talk
TALK, IDLE: bat chatter
TALK: tawk
TALKING: jawin'
TEA TOWEL: dish towel
TEETER TOTTER: seesaw
TEETH: nut crackers
TELL EM OFF: bless 'em out
TELL: tail
TEMPERATURE: temp-ture
TERRIBLE: teribl; turrable
TEXAS: Tex-is
THANK YOU: much abliged
THAT: at; thayet; thayet thair
THAT IS: at's
THAT THERE: at'air
THAT'S ALL: saul
THAT'S IT: acit
THAWED: unfroze it
THE: thu
THE END: preachin's over
THE OTHER: tuther
THEM: 'um
THERE: thay-ur
THICK: as Mississippi mud
THIGHS, BIG: thunder thighs
THIN: as hen skin
THING: thang
THINK: thank; cogitate
THINKS: thanks
THIRTEEN: thurt-tane
THIRTY: thurdy
THIS: this here
THIS WAY: this a way
THOSE ARE: them's
THOUGHT: racked my brain
THROAT: thote; gozzle
THROUGH: thoo
THROW: thow; chunk
TIGHT ONE: titan
TINY: tee-niney
TIRE: tar
TIRE IRON: tar arn

143

TIRED: tarred
TO: tuh
TOAD: toad frog
TOBACCO: tobaccer
TOILET: commode
TOLD: toll; tolt: toad
TOMATO: mater; love apple
TOMORROW: tamar
TONGUE-TIED: tie-tongued
TOSS: pitch
TOURISTS: comers and goers
TOWEL: tal
TOY: play pretty
TREE: tray
TRICKED: hoodwinked
TRUST: truss
TRYING: trine
TUESDAY: Twos-dee
TURN: time
TURNPIKE: innerstate
TURTLE: cooter
TWICE: twicet
TWINE: strang
UMPIRE: um-parr
UNCERTAIN: iffy
UNLESS: lessen
UNLIKE: unalike
UNUSUAL: beatenest
UPSET: tore up
URINAL: your-nul
USED TO: ewe-sta
UTILITY BILL: light bill
UTOPIA: hog heaven
VACUUM: dust sucker
VALLEY: holler
VALLEY, BIG: big holler
VARIOUS: var-us
VIADUCT: vye-duck
VICE VERSA: vicy versey
VIENNA SAUSAGE:
   vi-EEN-ers
VIOLIN: fiddle
VIRTUALLY: vurch-lee

VOWELS: vals
WAIT FOR: wait on
WALK: wahlk; hoof it
WALK QUIETLY: tippey toe
WALLOW: waller
WANT: wont
WANT TO: wanna
WANTED: wah'nid
WAREHOUSE: war haouse
WARM EMBRACE:
   all-squeezin hug
WAS: wuz
WASH CLOTH: warsh rag
WASH: warsh
WASHINGTON, DC: Warsh'n
   tun, Dee Sea
WASN'T: wudn't
WATCH FOR: Keep your eyes
   peeled
WATER, BAD: stale water
WATER, HOT: scaldin' hot
WATER: wadder; tap water
WATERMELON: wadder melon
WE WOULD HAVE: we'd da
WEAK: weakified
WELCOME SIGHT: sight for
   sore eyes
WELL: way-ul; whale
WENT CRAZY: spun a bearing
WEST: wayust
WHAT DID YOU SAY?: come
   again?
WHAT IF: s'posen
WHAT: whut
WHAT?: come again
WHATEVER: whatsomever
WHEELBARROW: we'ulbarah
WHERE: whayer; whur; where
   'bouts
WHERE IN HELL: war'n-hail
WHERE WILL: whirl
WHERE'D HE GO: where'd he
   slip off to

WHETSTONE: grindin' rock
WHICH WAY: which a way
WHILE: whilst
WHIP: whup; wear him out
WHIPPING: woodshed lecture
WHITE BACON: fat back
WHO: who all
WHOLE BUNCH: passel
WHOLESALE: hoe sale
WHORE HOUSE: cat house
WHY DON'T YOU: y-ont-cha
WIDOW: widar woman
WINDOW: win-da; winder
WINDY: airish
WINGS: wangs
WIRE: wahr
WISH: wisht
WISHBONE: pulley bone
WIT, DRY: rosin-jawed
WOLF: wuf
WOMAN: whoa-mun
WOMB: oven
WOMEN: wimmin folk
WOODCHUCK: ground hawg

WOODPECKER: peckerwood
WORM: war'm; wiggle tail;
  naight-crawler; red wiggler
WORN OUT: frazzled
WORSE: badder
WORSHIP: war-ship
WORST: sorriest
WORTHLESS: sorry
WOULD NOT: wooden
WRENCH: ranch
WRESTLING: ras-lin'
WRINKLES: knowledge lines
WRITER: ink slinger
YELL: beller; holler; squall;
  caterwaul
YELLOW: yell-ah or yell-er
YESTERDAY: yestiddty
YOU OUGHT TO: ya'otta
YOU WANT: y'ont
YOUNGSTER: youngun
YOUR: yore
ZERO: zee-row
ZINNIA: zeenia

SECTION THREE

Important Southern Stuff

FISHING LINE: Arkansas dental floss

Dixie, the Song

Dixie is the national anthem of the South despite the fact it was written, in 1859, in New York—New York City!—by Daniel Emmett, an Ohian who also wrote *Turkey in the Straw*. On March 4, 1861, prior to becoming the song of the South, *Dixie* was the song played during the grand march at the inaugural ball of one Abraham (Abra'damn) Lincoln. Anyone calling himself a Southerner ought to know the words:

> I wish I was in the land of cotton,
> old times there are not forgotten.
> Look away! Look away! Look away! Dixie Land.
> In Dixie Land where I was born in,
> early on one frosty morning,
> Look away! Look away! Look away Dixie Land.

> (Chorus)
> Then I wish I was in Dixie, Hooray! Hooray!
> In Dixie Land I'll take my stand,
> to live and die in Dixie.
> Away, away, away down south in Dixie.
> Away, away, away down south in Dixie.

> (Second verse)
> There's buckwheat cakes and Injun butter;
> Makes you fat or a little fatter.
> Look away! Look away! Look away Dixie Land.
> Then hoe it down and scratch your gravel:
> To Dixie Land I'm bound to travel.
> Look away! Look away! Look away Dixie Land.

> (Repeat chorus)

Dixie Protocol:

1. A true Southerner will stand reverently anywhere and anytime *Dixie* is played.

2. A devout Southerner will always remove his hat when *Dixie* is played, out of respect for the men who died for the cause.

3. Placing your right hand over your heart during playing of *Dixie* is optional except for the most devout Southerner.

4. Do not sing along unless you know the words.

Dixie, the place

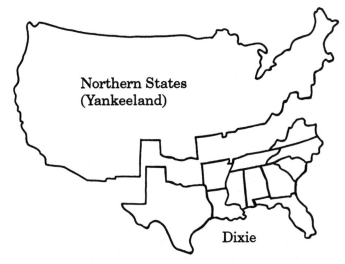

Dixie consists of the primary states that seceded from the Union during the War for Southern Rights. The following are the Dixie states and the capital cities:

Alabama	Montgomery
Arkansas	Little Rock
Florida	Tallahassee
Georgia	Atlanta
Louisiana	Baton Rouge
Mississippi	Jackson
North Carolina	Raleigh
South Carolina	Columbia
Texas	Austin
Tennessee	Nashville
Virginia	Richmond

In addition to the "big eleven" states, the leaders of the South wanted two more states to make a "magic thirteen." Missouri and Kentucky were officially admitted into the Confederacy, but neither state was ever totally committed to the cause and thus most Southerners recognize only the contributions of the "big eleven."

Manners, Southern Style

Always remove your toothpick before entering a restaurant.
Never clean the wax out of your ears with a car key in public.
Never ask anyone to hold your chew of tobacco.
Always offer to bait a lady's hook.
Never cuss before ladies, let them cuss first.
Never spit in a lady's waste basket or the church collection plate.
Remind granny to take out her snuff before she starts drinking.
Never correct one of granddaddy's stories.
Say ma'am and sir to your parents no matter how old you are.
Never relieve yourself off the porch unless it's your porch.
Clean your plate for your grandmother's sake.
When someone says "pass the biscuits" pass the entire plate.
Never wear your hat, chew tobacco, or snore in church.
Never refuse an invitation to visit a neighbor's garden.
Never track mud, blood, manure, or fish guts into the house.
Always wear clean underwear in case you're in an accident.
Leave your shoes on in a movie so others can enjoy it.
Stand when *Dixie* is played but only sing if you know the words.
Never complain about the food unless you cooked it.
Dance with who brung ya.
Always leave a light on for whoever ain't home yet.
Always have an alibi ready for kinfolk.
Never make fun of another person's dog, hat, or pickup.
Never tell a fishing story if any witnesses are present.
Never argue with a drunk, a skunk, or a red-headed woman.
Know where your ancestors are buried and never do anything to
cause 'em to spin in their graves.
Always be respectful of old dogs, old folks, and old whiskey.
Be kind to Yankees, they don't know no better.

Southern Terms of Endearment

Southerners have a special fondness for each other, especially
when they're sweet on each other. Here's some examples: Darlin'
• Sweet'art • Sugar Pie, Sugar Doodle, Sugar Lips, Sugar Plum,
Sugar Foot • Honey Bunch, Honey Bun, Honey Pie • Puddin',
Puddin' Pie, Puddin' Head • Pun'kin or Pun'kin Head • Dumplin'
• Buttercup • Sweetie Pie   *Note:* These terms should be
addressed to someone you know and not to casual strangers you
might meet in a honky tonk. Always remember, her real Honey
Bunch might be a line backer or deputy sheriff.

Southern Style Bumper Stickers

Southerners really like their bumper stickers, partially because bumper stickers tend to reflect the mind set. Here are some examples you may see on a Southern vehicle, especially a pickup:

Boycott Farmers: Don't Eat
Prune Juice Makes the Going Good
WARNING: Trespassers Will Be Violated
My Other Car is a Bass Boat
My Other Car is a John Deere
American by Birth, Southern by the Grace of God
If You Must Criticize Farmers, Don't Do It With Your Mouth Full
Hell No, I Ain't Forgettin'! (Printed next to a Rebel flag)
Rebel born, and Rebel bred; When I die, I'll be a Rebel dead
If you outlaw guns, only outlaws will have guns
Get Your Heart into America or Get Your Ass Out
Fishermen Do It With Long Rods
Jobs Are For People Who Don't Hunt or Fish
Have You Hugged Your Pickup Today?
Pass With Care, Driver Chews Tobacco!
Fish Naked
Coon Hunters Do It in the Woods
Bass Fishermen are a Great Catch
Elvis Lives
My Mother-in-Law's Car is a Broom
Manure Makes Crops and Government Grow
This Vehicle Stops at all Hog Crossings
If You Can Read This, Back Off
I'd Rather Be at a Honky Tonk
Yankee Go Home
Guns Don't Kill People, People Kill People
I ain't a cowboy, I just found the hat
In trouble? Call a Hippie
God made Southerners; The rest came from Sears
Chips Happen
Gun control is bein' able to hit what you aim at
Rebel Power
Get Your Head in America or get Your Butt Out
Vote for What's His Name
We don't give a damn how you did it up North!

Proverbs, Southern Style

Use it up, wear it out; make it do, or do without.
The difference between picking corn and cotton is the amount of stooping.
The biggest fish are caught by the tale.
Friendship is like a dollar, hard to get, easy to throw away.
The best stove wood is the stove wood that is farthest away.
Good fences make good neighbors.
It ain't broke so don't fix it.
Cut your own firewood and it'll warm you twice.
If you don't think too good, don't think too often.
If you don't make dust, you eat it.
Never let the seeds keep you from enjoying the watermelon.
If you don't bite, don't growl.
A new tune can be played on an old fiddle.
Big men leave deep tracks.
A loaded wagon creaks; an empty one rattles.
If you grab a bull's tail, you'll see horns.
Even a black cow gives white milk.
A good scare is worth more than good advice.
Don't try to get all the coons up one tree.
If you give a cow a choice, she'll go out the wrong gate.
If you put all your eggs in one basket, watch that basket.
If your dog ain't home, he's botherin' the neighbors.
Given the choice of bein' a hammer or a nail, be the hammer.
Whether you're in the fryin' pan or the fire, you still get burned.
Always watch your step when the chips are down.
It's better to plow around a stump then through it.
You gotta pluck the chicken before you fry it.
It's better to wear out than to rust out.
A wishbone is no substitute for a backbone.
Don't sell the bear skin 'till you kill the bear.
If you can't help, don't hinder.
Burnin' daylight don't keep you warm.
A narrow minded person is like a long-necked bottle; the less he has in him the more noise it makes coming out.
Every dog knows the difference between bein' stumbled over and bein' kicked.
Sometimes you're the windshield; sometimes you're the bug.
Every ol' hog likes to hear himself grunt.

Other Regional Books From Wordware

100 Days in Texas: The Alamo Letters
by Wallace O. Chariton

The Battlefields of Texas
by Kevin R. Young and Dr. Stephen Hardin

**Classic Clint: The Laughs and Times
of Clint Murchison, Jr.**
by Dick Hitt

**Country Savvy: Survival Tips for Farmers,
Ranchers, and Cowboys**
by Reed Blackmon

Critter Chronicles
by Jim Dunlap

Dirty Dining: A Cookbook, and More, for Lovers
by Ginnie Siena Bivona

**Don't Throw Feathers at Chickens: A Collection of
Texas Political Humor**
by Charles Herring, Jr. and Walter Richter

Exploring the Alamo Legends
by Wallace O. Chariton

The Final Exam on Texas Trivia
by Wallace O. Chariton

The Great Texas Airship Mystery
by Wallace O. Chariton

Hardin's Pardon
by Dr. Stephen Hardin

Kingmakers
by John R. Knaggs

Rainy Days in Texas Funbook
by Wallace O. Chariton

Rattling Around in Texas
by Jim Dunlap

**Recovery: A Directory to Texas Substance Abuse
Treatment Facilities**
Edited by Linda Manning Miller

Other Regional Books From Wordware

The Rise and Fall of the Alamo
by Thomas Lindley

San Antonio Uncovered
by Mark Louis Rybczyk

Spirits of San Antonio and South Texas
by Docia Schultz Williams

Texas: An Owner's Manual
by Wallace O. Chariton

Texas Highway Humor
by Wallace O. Chariton

Texas Politics in My Rearview Mirror
by Waggoner Carr with Byron Varner

Texas Tales Your Teacher Never Told You
by Charles F. Eckhardt

Texas Wit and Wisdom
by Wallace O. Chariton

That Cat Won't Flush
by Wallace O. Chariton

That Old Overland Stagecoaching
by Eva Jolene Boyd

They Don't Have to Die
by Jim Dunlap

This Dog'll Hunt
by Wallace O. Chariton

To the Tyrants Never Yield
by Kevin R. Young

A Trail Rider's Guide to Texas
by Mary Elizabeth Sue Goldman

Unsolved Texas Mysteries
by Wallace O. Chariton

Also check your local bookstore for fine computer books from
Wordware Publishing, Inc.